# The Believer's Absolute Surrender

# The Believer's Absolute Surrender

## Andrew Murray

## BETHANY HOUSE PUBLISHERS

MINNEAPOLIS, MINNESOTA 55438
A Division of Bethany Fellowship, Inc.

Published by Bethany House Publishers
A Division of Bethany Fellowship, Inc.
6820 Auto Club Road, Minneapolis, Minnesota 55438

Printed in the United States of America

**Library of Congress Cataloging in Publication Data**

Murray, Andrew, 1828–1917.
    The believer's absolute surrender.

    (The Andrew Murray Christian maturity library)
    Rev. ed. of: Absolute surrender.
    1. Christian life.   I. Murray, Andrew, 1828–1917.
Absolute surrender.   II. Title.   III. Series.
BV4501.M796    1985         248.2         85–447
ISBN 0–87123–827–6 (pbk.)

# *Books by Andrew Murray*

ANDREW MURRAY was born in South Africa in 1828. After receiving his education in Scotland and Holland, he returned to that land and spent many years there as both pastor and missionary. He was a staunch advocate of biblical Christianity. He is best known for his many devotional books.

# Contents

# Introduction

By way of introduction, it should be noted that the following chapters were originally sermons which I delivered at the Keswick Convention. For those readers who may never have attended such a convention, I need to clarify the special reason for which the messages were first spoken and are now published.

The explanation is found quickly by pointing to the origin of the Keswick Convention. Canon Battersby had for more than twenty years been an earnest evangelical minister, known and recognized as a godly man. But that godliness bore in his heart the common mark of today's believer—the consciousness of not living well-pleasing to God. The painful sense of continual failure and defeat in the battle with sin, the frequent loss of the light and joy of God's presence, made the perfect peace and abiding fellowship of which the Word speaks an impossibility. Before the great Oxford Convention of 1874, he had been deeply stirred by the news that some there would testify of victory over sin and continuous walking in the light as the rule of their Christian experience. He saw that there were promises in God's Word to warrant this, but he did not know how to receive them. At the convention he heard a message on faith as *a resting on Christ's Word*, and saw that by faith he could claim and receive the power of Christ to do in him what he had thought before as impossible. The Spirit of God opened his understanding to see this, and confirmed this great fact in him, and at once he was ready to testify of what God had done for him.

The Keswick Convention had its origin in the desire to give this testimony in wider circles. He spoke with others of the old life they too had lived, of the new life and joy God had now given, and of the simple way in which through faith they had found the passage from the one to the other. The blessing that followed was great. Many who were longing for a holy life found the help they needed. In the power and joy of the Holy Spirit an atmosphere was created, of which the presence is felt even as I write. The intensely personal call to confession and surrender of what was wrong in the past, the joyous testimony of what Christ has made possible, and the uncomplicated appeal to come and by a single act of faith prove at once God's faithfulness and power, brought a message and a blessing that many had never heard or thought possible.

And why have I written this? My reason is to point out and press home upon my readers the three great thoughts which mark these conventions and which these chapters attempt to illustrate.

Their first aim is always to uncover the evil lie that a carnal Christian life is all that is possible. Nothing does more harm in the Body of Christ than the secret thought that obedience is impossible. Until believers see the error of this, and honestly view their life of continual failure as sinful and unallowable, no preaching will help. The first lesson must be that to walk after the flesh with a continually yielding to self-will is contrary to what God absolutely requires and actually gives.

The second aim of this teaching is to make clear that God has in reality made a provision in Christ, the almighty Savior from sin, and in the Holy Spirit dwelling in us, by which the life of victory and rest and fellowship can be maintained. Christ in His saving power can be real within us moment by moment. It is only as we see in God's Word this life prepared for us that we can have the courage to hope for it.

Then comes the third point, that the transition from the old life of stumbling and broken fellowship can be made in a moment by one decisive step. And this is possible because it is nothing more than a new act of faith in Christ, trusting Him to work in us what we have failed to do ourselves.

I urgently request the reader to regard this book as a very simple personal appeal. Ask God to deal with you and to show you whether you are walking in that path of absolute surrender and close fellowship to which you are called. If you read the book as a scholar, to gather more truths into notebooks, or as one simply desiring to be edified, you will very likely be disappointed. But if you read it as one desiring deliverance from sin, you will very likely be blessed.

With the humble prayer that God may by His Spirit bless the written page, as it has pleased Him to bless the spoken word when we were gathered in His presence, I commit the book and its readers to His holy care.

Andrew Murray
Wimbledon
December 2, 1895

# 1

## *Be Filled with the Spirit*

These well-known words about the Holy Spirit are found in Acts 2:4, *"They were all filled with the Holy Ghost,"* and in Ephesians 5:18, *"Be filled with the Spirit."* The one text is a narrative; it tells us what actually happened. The other is a command; it tells us what we should be. In case there is any doubt about it actually being a command, we find it linked to another command, "Be not drunk with wine . . . but *be filled with the Spirit."*

Now, I am sure that if I asked you, Do you try to obey the command "to not be drunk with wine"? you would answer immediately, "Of course, as a believer, I obey that command." But now, how about the other—"Be filled with the Spirit," have you obeyed that command? Is that the life you are living? If not, the question comes at once, Why not? And then the next question, Are you willing to take up that command and say, "By God's help I am going to obey. I will not rest until I have obeyed that command, until I am filled with the Spirit"?

From the very beginning, we must limit ourselves to the simple question of listening to the command of God's Holy Spirit in His Word. For the moment we want to put away our varying notions and conceptions about the filling of the Holy Spirit. We want to press in on the realization of the one special object we are now aiming at and the message we believe

13

God has for every believer: "My child, I want you filled with the Spirit." Let your answer be: "Father, I want it too; I am ready; I yield myself to obey my God; let me be filled with your Spirit now."

And to clarify what it is to be filled with the Spirit, let me say that it does not mean a state of high excitement, or of absolute perfection, or a state in which there will be no growth. No. Being filled with the Spirit is simply this—having my whole personality yielded to His power. When the whole soul is yielded to the Holy Spirit, God himself will fill it.

Now the question comes, *What is needed in order to be filled with the Spirit?* The question is of the utmost importance, and if we would find the answers we must allow God to search our lives. We sing the hymn that God might *search* us, and that searching will help us to look into our heart and life and say: Am I in the condition in which God can fill me with the Spirit? As God answers, some of you may be able to honestly say: Thank God, I am ready. You may then perhaps see that you have been kept back from this full blessing by some ignorance, or prejudice, or unbelief, or wrong thoughts of what it is.

It seems that the best place to find the answer to our question is to look at the way in which Christ prepared the disciples for the Day of Pentecost. It reminds us of what is done in heathen lands where the missionary preaches. Converts come to him and he forms a baptismal class. He sometimes trains these young converts for a year or longer, to educate and test them, and to prepare them for the Christian life. Jesus had His disciples three years in His baptismal class, and they went through a time of training and preparation. It was not magic, not an arbitrary thing, that the Holy Spirit came upon them. They were prepared for it. John the Baptist told them what was to come. He not only preached the Lamb of God who was to shed His blood, but he preached— and he tells us that it was by special revelation from God— that He on whom John saw the Holy Spirit descend would baptize with the Holy Spirit.

So what did the training of those disciples consist of? How were they prepared for the baptism of the Holy Spirit?

First of all, remember that *they were men who had forsaken all to follow Jesus.* Jesus went to the one and said, "Forsake your net"; and to another, "Leave that place in the receipt of custom, and come and follow Me." They did and could afterwards say by the mouth of Peter, "Lord, we have forsaken all and followed thee"—their homes, their families, their good name. Men mocked and laughed at them, men called them *the disciples of Jesus,* and when He was despised and hated they were hated too. They identified themselves with Him; they utterly yielded themselves to do His bidding. This is the first step in the way to the baptism of the Holy Spirit. We must forsake all to follow Christ.

I am not now speaking about forsaking *sin*; that you have to do when you are converted. But there is something that has a far wider meaning. Many believers think that they receive Jesus as someone who can save them and help them, yet all but deny Him as Master. They think they have a right to have their own will in a thousand things. They speak very much what they want, they do very much what they like, they use their property and possessions as they desire; they are their own masters and have never dreamed of saying: "Jesus, I forsake all to follow You."

And yet this is the command of Christ. Christ as Lord of all infinite riches and glory deserves it, and He is such a heavenly, spiritual, divine gift that unless we yield everything, our hearts cannot be filled with Him. Jesus' words have not changed: "Forsake all and follow Me."

Recently I was at Johannesburg and heard a simple story of what has been done there in God's kingdom. At a gathering of believers to testify of what God had done for them, a woman rose and told how, some six months before, she had received such a wonderful blessing through the inflowing of God's Spirit. At a consecration meeting, the minister had asked who were ready to yield themselves entirely to Jesus. He used the words, "Suppose He wanted you to go to China, or to give up your wife and children, would you be willing to do it?" And she said earnestly, "I *did* want to say, I will give up everything to Jesus, but I could not. When he asked those who were willing to rise, I was under great conviction; nevertheless, I rose and said: 'Yes, I will give up everything.' Yet I felt as if I could not give up my husband and children. I went home, but I could not sleep; I could not rest, for there was the struggle; must I give up *everything*? I *wanted* to do it for the sake of Jesus. It was past midnight, and I said: 'Lord, yes, for You *everything*! And the joy and the power of the Spirit flowed into my heart.' " She testified, and her minister testified of her too, that now she walked in the joy of the Lord.

Perhaps you have never said the same or never thought it was needed. Are you willing to say, "O Christ, let me be filled with the Holy Spirit; I will give up anything and everything; receive my surrender"?

Each of us must examine ourselves. Some have never thought it a necessity to do it. Some have never understood what it meant when Jesus said that unless a man hate father and mother, and wife and children, and houses and lands, and forsake them for His sake and the gospel's, he is not worthy of Him. Surely this is the reason for your lack of victory over sin, the reason that the Holy Spirit does not fill your being—you have never forsaken all to follow Christ.

A second thought to consider: They were not only men who had forsaken all to follow Jesus, but they were *intensely attached to Him*. Jesus had said, "If ye love me, keep my commandments. And I will pray the Father, and he will give you another Comforter." And they *did* love Him intensely. They had seen Him crucified, but their hearts could not be separated from Him. They had no hope or joy or comfort on earth without Him; and this is what is so often lacking among us. We trust Jesus and His work on Calvary; we trust Him as our only Savior; that is sufficient to bring us salvation. But there is the relationship of an intense, close, personal attachment to Jesus and fellowship with Him every day—

the relationship that means that Jesus, the unseen One, shall be my Friend and Guide and Keeper all the day, my Leader and Master whom I obey. But alas! how few understand these thoughts!

This is one of the strong elements of the "Keswick teaching." A few years ago a young missionary came out to South Africa and spoke so often of the blessing she had received at Keswick. She told me that as a child she had loved the Lord Jesus and had been educated in a circle of godly friends and a godly home, but what a difference it had made when she found what it is to receive the deeper blessing. I said to her, "You have from your childhood lived in a bright, godly atmosphere; what do you think is the difference between the life you then lived and the life you have entered into?" Her quick answer was simple and bright. "It is just this," she said, *"the personal fellowship of Jesus."*

Oh, believer, this must be the beginning of the deeper blessing. Some people would forsake everything for the sake of their religion. For a false religion multitudes have given up all. Some would forsake all for the sake of their church. Some people would forsake all for the sake of their fellowmen. But that is not what is wanted. We want to forsake all for the sake of Jesus, to let Him come into our life and take possession of our heart. Is your life one of tender personal attachment to Jesus and of joy in Him? I am not asking if your love is perfect, but I am asking if you can say honestly: It is what I am striving after, it is what I have yielded myself to, it is what I long for above everything. Jesus Christ must have me every day and all the day.

A third thought: These disciples were *men who had been led to despair of themselves.* At the beginning of their three years of instruction they had to give up all they possessed; but it was only at the end of that time that they began to give up themselves. They had given up their nets, their homes, their friends, and that was right; but throughout the three years how strong self was! How often Jesus spoke to them about humility! But they could not understand Him.

Time after time there was contention between them as to who should be chief. The night before the crucifixion they were still arguing over it. They had not given up self. It was obvious to all how little they lived in the Spirit of Jesus!

But Christ taught them and trained them. He revealed to them, time after time, what the sin of pride is, and what the glory of humility is so that when He died upon the cross, they died a terrible death too. Think of Peter, the impetuous disciple, having denied his Lord. Don't you think that in all the sorrows of those three days, from the crucifixion day to the resurrection day, the deepest and the bitterest was this—shame at the thought of how he had treated his Lord? Then he learned to despair of himself. At the Supper table how self-confident he had been! "Although all men shall be offended . . . yet will I never be offended." But Jesus took him down with Him into death and the grave, and then Peter knew that there was in him, indeed, no good thing. He had learned to despair of himself.

Some of you may say: I think I have given up all for Jesus; my property, my home, my friends, my position, and I think I do love Him, but I still have not received the blessing. Dear friend, are you willing that God, with His searchlight, would uncover in you how much there is of self-will and self-trust? Take, for instance, your judgment of people; how you speak just what you like and what you think right, and have not yet learned to study the humility and tenderness and gentleness of Jesus. That is *self*. You work for Him. You try to do good, but all the time it is really your own working. You are doing the work, and you look to God to help and bless. But that cannot be. God must first bring each one of us down into the place of death.

Do you know what the death of Jesus means? It means this—that Jesus said to His Father, in effect: Here is My life, so precious to Me, My life which has been sinless. I have yielded it to You in life, but now I am going to yield it to You in death. He went into the grave saying, "Into thy hands I commit"—I give away, I entrust—"my spirit." And you know what happened. Because He gave up His life so entirely, and sank into the thick darkness of death and the grave, God raised Him up into a new life and a new glory. It was the death that was the secret of the resurrection. And, believer, understand that if you want to be filled with the Spirit and the risen life of glory, you must first die to self. The apostles were men who had been brought to an utter self-despair, men who had lost all, and who were ready to receive all from God in heaven.

A fourth thought: These apostles were *men who had accepted the promise of the Spirit from Jesus in faith*. On the night before the crucifixion Christ had spoken to them about the Holy Spirit more than once, and when He was ready to ascend, He said again, "Ye shall be baptized with the Holy Ghost not many days hence." If you had asked those disciples, What does that mean? I am sure they could not have told you. They had no conception of what would come. But they took the word of Jesus, and if they had any need for talking or arguing during those ten days, I am sure they said: If while He was on earth He did such wonderful things for us, now that He is in glory He will do things infinitely more wonderful. And they waited for that.

You, too, must accept this promise by faith and say: "The promise of the filling of the Holy Spirit is for *me*. I accept it at the hand of Jesus." You may not understand it; you may not feel as you would like to feel; you may feel weak and sinful and far from Jesus; but you may say—and you have a right to say it—the promise is for *me*. Are you ready to do so? Are you ready in faith to trust the promise, and the word, and the love of Jesus?

I am sure there are believers who are struggling to find out where they are lacking, who possibly have yielded themselves most heartily and fully to Jesus, who do love Him, who have sought to humble themselves in the dust. But the problem is that they have not learned to simply say: He has promised, and He will do it.

Let me say, for your encouragement, that when you get a promise from God it is worth just as much as a fulfillment.

A promise brings you into direct contact with God. Honor Him by trusting the promise and obeying Him, and if there is any preparation that you still need, God knows about it; and if there is anything that is to be opened up to you He will do it if you count upon Him to do it. Trust the promise and say, "This fullness of the Holy Spirit is for me."

And then, the last thought about the disciples is this: *On the strength of that promise they waited in united prayer.* And that is what we must do—wait on God in prayer. They waited, they prayed with one accord; prayer and supplication went up to God mingled with praise. They expected—our primary lesson—God in heaven to do something. I wish I could stress the importance of that! I find believers—and I have found it in my own experience—who read, and understand, and think, and wish, and want to claim, and want to take, and want to get, and yet what they desire eludes their grasp. Why? Because they do not wait for God to give it.

Do not look to a teaching or to what you think and understand, with the idea of receiving a blessing from it. *Look to God and expect God to do something.* It is not enough to believe. I find that many people mistake their personal faith for the blessing that faith is intended to bring. By faith I am to "inherit the promises." Oh, believe and trust God; then look to Him to give the blessing. Be "filled with the Holy Ghost."

# 2

# *The Blessedness of Being Filled with the Spirit*

My purpose is to try to put before you the blessedness of a life filled with the Holy Spirit. We clarified the way in which the disciples were led to receive the blessing; now let us look at their blessedness in being filled with the Spirit. It may please God to make our desire so strong, and to make us see so clearly, *This is just what I need, I cannot live any longer without it,* that He may bring us to receive more than we ever expected. He is a God who is willing and able to do above what we can ask or think.

The clearest illustration of the joy and blessedness of being filled with the Spirit is seen in the wonderful change which Pentecost made in the lives of the disciples. It is one of the most wonderful object lessons in the whole of Scripture—those twelve men under Christ's training for three years, and yet remaining, apparently, at such a distance from the life they were meant to live; and then all at once, by the blessed incoming of the Holy Spirit, being made just what God wanted them to be.

Look first at *the change that Pentecost brought into their relationship with Jesus.* During His earthly ministry Jesus could not live within them. He was outside, separated from them—very near, very loving; and yet, if I may say so with deep reverence, what a failure Christ's teaching was to them until the Holy Spirit came! Christ taught them humility time after time. He said, "Learn of me, for I am meek and lowly in heart," and "He that humbleth himself shall be exalted." Yet right up to the end they were still contending which of them was greatest.

Christ did not conquer their pride. This was not due to lack of divine teaching. Why was it, then? It was because of one thing: Christ was still outside them and could not get into their hearts to dwell. It was impossible; the time had not come, and thus they had only the divine, almighty, blessed Redeemer alongside them, but still outside. And how different they were from Him! It teaches us that no outward instruction, even from Christ himself or His words in Scripture, can bring us the true and full blessing until the Holy Spirit works it in us.

But what a change took place on the Day of Pentecost! "At that day ye shall know that I am in you." What does that mean? Christ in us, just like we are reading in a room? No, we are in the room, but we can go out of it again and not suffer anything by it. I can leave the room and go elsewhere. The room and I are not vitally, organically connected. But the Lord Jesus came to be—I say it with reverence—part of those disciples, to fill their hearts and thoughts and affections; and what Peter and James and John had when they had Christ alongside them, you and I have in a much larger measure, if we have the living Christ within us.

And how did that change come? By the Holy Spirit. "At that day"—when the Spirit comes—"you shall know that I am in you; for the Father will love you, and I will love you, and we will come and make our abode in you."

Oh! isn't that what your heart longs for? I have thought and thought of Jesus in Bethlehem, of Jesus on Calvary, of Jesus upon the throne, and I have worshiped and loved and rejoiced exceedingly in Him; but all the time I wanted something better, something deeper and something nearer. The answer is to have the living Jesus within. That is what the

Holy Spirit will give you, and that is why we plead with you. Will you not yield yourself to receive this blessing—to be filled with the Spirit—that the blessed Jesus may be able to take possession of you? Is not that what your heart longs for? Jesus *within*—the very Jesus, who is the almighty One, who died on the cross and sits upon the throne, condescending to be your life?

That is what the Spirit comes for. Jesus said, "He shall glorify me: for he shall receive of mine and shall show it unto you." And what is the glory of Jesus? His love and His power. The Holy Spirit will reveal Christ in us, so that the wonderful love of Christ shall be a possession and a reality in its divine nearness, and that power of Christ shall have the mastery within us. You know the wonderful prayer in Ephesians three, that the Father might strengthen them with might by the Spirit in the inner man, that Christ might dwell in their hearts. The mighty power of the Holy Spirit can do it. The Holy Spirit makes Jesus present within us.

Furthermore, not only was Jesus outside of them, but He was not always with them. They could not be with Him every moment. You remember that He sent them across the sea while He stayed on the mountain to pray. You remember that He took three of them with Him up into the mountain, but the others stayed below; and there they had to meet the Pharisees and could not cast out the evil spirit. There were times of separation and at last there came that terrible death, that awful separation from the world. Yes, Christ was their life—sometimes with Christ, and sometimes not with Him; sometimes near Him, and sometimes the crowd pressing around Him, and they could not get to Him.

But, ah! friends, *the presence of Jesus by the Holy Spirit is meant to be unbroken, continual, and forever.* Is not that what your heart longs for? Perhaps you know what it is like to live a week or a month in a joy that makes your heart sing all the day. Then the change comes with the cloud and the darkness—and you do not know why it is—sometimes with bodily sickness or depression, sometimes with the cares and the difficulties of this life, sometimes with the consciousness of your own failure. Oh, that I could convince every believer correctly! Jesus does love you; He does not wish to be separated from you for a minute. He cannot bear it. We want to believe in that love of Jesus. No mother has ever so delighted in the baby she has in her arms as does the Christ of God delight in you. He wants both intimate and unceasing fellowship with you. Receive it, beloved believer, and say: "If it is possible, God helping me, I must have this filling of the Holy Spirit, that I may have Jesus always dwelling in my heart."

Second, *notice the change Pentecost made in their own inner life.* Until then, theirs was a life of failure and weakness. I have spoken of their pride. Christ had to reprove them for their pride repeatedly. You know how they longed to be faithful to Him, yet their pride and self-confidence were the cause of continual failure. Peter said, "Lord, I will never deny thee," and all the others said the same; yet, within a few hours they denied Him—the result of pride and self-confidence. They did not know the evil within them. Jesus had done everything to teach them humility, but He could not change their inner weakness. Peter had said, "I will go with thee to prison and to death," but at the word of a maidservant he began to swear and to declare that he never knew the Man. What utter weakness!

But what a change when Pentecost came! I will not say they had victory over sin, for I do not think it came in the way of direct fighting. But when the Holy Spirit—the Spirit of God—became their life, they were filled with the might and the power of the living Jesus, the Savior from sin.

You know that the great work of Jesus is to take away sin. And how does He take it away? Many believers just look upon Him as taking it away on the cross. Others get a step further and say: He takes it away from heaven; He cleanses and keeps me. But the true taking away of sin is this: If the light comes in, the darkness is expelled. It is the presence of Jesus, indwelling by the Holy Spirit, that makes us holy. And the disciples—what a change came over them! Notice how boldly they were able to speak in the presence of those who threatened them with death. "We must obey God rather than men," they said. They went to prison and there sang praises to God at midnight. Oh, the wonderful change in their life the Holy Spirit wrought!

And what does that teach us? We very often speak about the self-life and the life of the Holy Spirit. Have you said to God—perhaps you have said it often—"Lord, how can I be rid of this self-life?" Well, has God answered you? Has God's finger reached into the deep place of your heart and brought you to say, "O God, my failure is my own self-confidence, self-will, self-pleasing"? The accursed self will have its say in everything, and there is no power that can expel that but the power of the presence of Jesus.

Don't get entangled in theological definitions as to how it is all done or as to how much sin there remains or how much is cast out. Be content that though you cannot completely explain and expound it, you still believe that the Spirit of holiness which will be given is the holiness of Jesus in your heart. Filled with the Spirit, you have within you the power of the holiness of God to do the blessed work of sanctification.

Third, *the filling of the Holy Spirit changed the disciples' relationship with one another.* Look at *the love that united them into one body.* Before, we mentioned that there was selfishness among them, often a lack of love; but when the Holy Spirit came—do not look only at what He did for each one of them individually—He molded them into one body. They knew they were the members of one Lord Jesus, and because of their love for each other they did things which were utterly unheard of at that time. Though most of them were strangers, they began to sell their goods and give away their property, and to say they had all things in common. This was the result of the Holy Spirit having come down, as the very love of God in heaven, to dwell in their hearts.

Perhaps you find that your greatest difficulty in life is your relationship with other believers? Very often, people who have to work together differ in temperament and character, and how easily friction comes in! Then there are people who differ in regard to some theological truth or practical way of doing Christ's work, and how they speak or write against each other! Alas, what separations there are in Christ's Church on earth! Even among those who profess to love God, and profess holiness and entire consecration, what divisions unceasingly come! It is such a sad thing. There are so many earnest believers who have so much to say about others! They can point out where I am wrong, and I can point out where they are wrong; but how few there are who though distinctly differing with each other can still say, "Above all our differences there is a unity which we must express; we want continual fellowship in the presence of our one Father."

Do you want to have a heart overflowing with love to every believer, even to those outside your own circle? Do you want a heart of love that can set others on fire? Do you want the very love of heaven to flow out from you? Do you want the self-sacrificing love of Jesus to take possession of you, so that you can bear and forbear, so that with the longsuffering and tenderness and gentleness, and the very meekness of Christ, the Lamb of God, you are willing to be the helper and servant of everyone, however unlovable or unlovely? Then you need to be filled with the Spirit. Cry for that, claim that, accept that, rest not until you have it. The Spirit is the Spirit of God's love, the Spirit of the crucified love of Jesus. If we receive the Holy Spirit, the love of God will be shed abroad in our hearts, and God will melt us into one as never before.

And then fourth, *the coming of the Holy Spirit changed their works.* What a difference Pentecost made! And I suppose we all feel—at least many of us feel—that that is one of the important things in connection with speaking about being filled with the Holy Spirit. Many Christian workers thank God for the way He has led them on, but still feel that they are lacking something. They lack both the continual joy in speaking about Jesus and the consciousness that God is using them as one of His instruments. Yet that is what God wants every worker to have. How many Sunday school teachers and Bible study leaders feel this way: "I am not confident, not equipped, ignorant, but I know my God is using me, for I have given myself into His hands, and I have consented to be anything for Him. I never mind, though my work is powerless and I sometimes feel ashamed of it, for I have put myself into God's hands as an instrument for Him to use"?

Would it not be unutterable joy to always work in that spirit of absolute humility and dependence, with a childlike trust that God will use you? How are you to get that? Look at the apostles, look at the disciples. I read that Jesus sent them out to do three things: to preach the gospel, to heal the sick, and to cast out demons. When they came back they told about the last two—healing the sick and the casting out demons; but I do not hear them tell about conversions. I do not think their preaching of the gospel really helped very much. It had to be done, but I do not know that it resulted in much.

But when the Day of Pentecost came, listen to their preaching of the gospel—not only to Peter's; they were all proclaiming the mighty works of God. What a blessing came! And it went on and on. What a boldness they had and what largeness of heart! They went on to Samaria and to Caesarea, and then to Antioch, and there waited upon God; within a very few years the gospel had been brought into Europe! It was the power of the Holy Spirit that did it. Here we lack the power for our work, whether it is the large fields of missions or even in our immediate neighborhood.

I thank God for all the interest He is awakening for the lost and foreign missions, but I am afraid there is something remaining neglected. And what is that? I thank God for all the interest there is in working with the poor and the neglected, with the drunkards and those who are in danger of becoming drunkards, and with the poor outcasts. But your middle classes, your richer and higher classes—is there power in your Christianity to take the gospel to them boldly? Are not many of you members of churches and congregations, where you sit Sunday by Sunday with multitudes around you, of whom you know many are unconverted? Is there not a need of divine wisdom and power to equip us for this work? Do we not need divine light and inspiration? Do we not need power, with a new love and boldness to pray and wait and work, and to see that not only those who are in China, or in Africa, or in other parts shall have the gospel, but that the gospel shall be brought to those with whom we are associated every day? We thank God that during the last years He has aroused Christians to work as never before; but let us understand that it is but a beginning. If believers will hold counsel with God, wait upon Him in prayer and say that they are ready for His work, is not God able to do far more than He has accomplished so far?

Only one thing is needed. The Spirit did it all—on the Day of Pentecost and afterward. It was the Spirit who gave the boldness, the wisdom, the message, and the converting power.

I speak to every believer who feels the need of power. Is not your whole heart ready to say that this is what you want? "I see it. Jesus did not send me to the warfare on my own orders; He does not ask me to go and preach and teach in my own strength; Jesus meant me to have the fullness of the Holy Spirit, whether I am at home teaching my children or afar on mission work. Whether I have a little Sunday school class or some larger work, the one thing I need is the power of the Holy Spirit, to be filled with the Spirit."

Let me conclude by asking, Are you prepared now to receive this from our Jesus? He loves to give it. God delights in nothing so much as to honor His Son, and it is honor to Jesus when souls are filled with the Holy Spirit because then He proves what He can do for them. Shall we not claim it?

Let me give you four words as steps. Let everyone who longs for this blessing say, first of all, "*I must be filled*." Say it to God in the depth of your heart. "God commands it; I cannot live my life as I should without it."

Then say, as the second step, "*I may be filled*. It is possible that promise is for me." Settle that and let all doubt vanish.

The apostles, once so full of pride and self-life, were filled with the Holy Spirit because they took hold of Jesus. And, with all your sinfulness, if you will but cling to Him, you *may be filled.*

Then, thirdly, say, *"I would be filled."* To get the "pearl of great price" you must sell all, you must give up everything. You are willing, are you not? "Everything, Lord, if I may only have that. Lord, I would have it from You now."

And then comes the last step. *"I shall be filled.* God longs to give it; I shall have it." Never mind whether it comes as a flood or in deep silence; or whether it does not come now because God is preparing you for it tomorrow. But say, *"I shall be filled.* If I entrust myself to Jesus, He cannot disappoint me." It is His very nature, it is His work in heaven, it is His delight to give souls the Holy Spirit in full measure. Oh, claim it now: "My God, it is so solemn, it is almost awful; it is too blessed and too true—Lord, will You not do it? My trembling heart says, *I shall be filled* with the Holy Spirit." Oh, say to God, *"Father, I shall,* for the name of my Savior is Jesus, who saves from all sin, and who fills with the Holy Spirit. Glory to His name!"

# 3

# *Carnal and Spiritual*

Our thoughts in this chapter will center around 1 Corinthians 3:1–4: *"And I, brethren, could not speak unto you as unto spiritual, but as unto carnal, even as unto babes in Christ."* The Apostle begins the chapter by telling the Corinthians that there are two levels of Christian living. Some believers are *carnal,* some are *spiritual.* By the discernment of the Holy Spirit, Paul saw that the Corinthians were carnal, and he wanted to tell them so. You will find the word *carnal* four times in these four verses.

Paul felt that all his preaching would be useless if he talked about spiritual things to men who were unspiritual. They were believers, real Christians, babes in Christ; but there was one deadly fault—they were *carnal.* He seems to say: I cannot teach you spiritual truth about the spiritual life; you cannot receive it. It was not because they were stupid. They were very clever and full of knowledge, but unable to understand spiritual teaching. Thus, this simple lesson— all the trouble among believers who sometimes receive a blessing and lose it again is because they are *carnal;* if we want to keep the blessing, we must become *spiritual.* We must choose which level of Christian life we desire—the *carnal* life or the *spiritual.* Choose the *spiritual* and God will be delighted to give it to you.

To understand this teaching we must begin by trying to

thoroughly explain what the carnal state is. I will point out four very marked characteristics of the carnal state.

The *first* thing is that *the carnal state is a state of protracted infancy.* A long time has passed since you were converted. By this time you should be a young man, but you are still a babe in Christ. "I have fed you with milk, and not with meat; for hitherto ye were not able to bear it." You know how a baby is, and what a beautiful thing babyhood is. Is there anything more delightful than a six-month-old child, with ruddy cheeks, laughing and smiling face, kicking little feet, and moving of little fingers? What beauty! But suppose I saw the same child six months later and he was not a bit bigger. The parents would say, "We are afraid there is something the matter; the child isn't growing." If after three years I saw that the baby was still no bigger, I would find the parents sad. They would tell me, "The doctor says he has a terrible disease and cannot grow. He says it's a wonder he's alive." Ten years later there is still no growth.

You see, babyhood at the proper time is the most beautiful thing in the world, but babyhood continued too long is a burden and a sorrow, a sign of disease or disorder. And that was the state of many of the Corinthian believers. They continued as babies.

Now, what are the marks of a baby? A baby cannot help itself, and cannot help others. That is the life of many believers. They make their ministers into spiritual nursemaids. It is a serious matter when spiritual babies keep their ministers continuously occupied in nursing and feeding them, and they never help themselves. They do not know how to feed on Christ's Word; the minister must feed them. They do not know what contact with God is; the minister must pray for them. They do not know what it is to live as those who have God to help them; they always want to be nursed. Is that the reason why *you* go to church—to get your nurses to give you spiritual meat? God be praised for the preaching of the gospel and for the fellowship of believers. But, you know what a baby does. He always occupies somebody. You cannot leave him alone. Likewise, there are many spiritual infants to whom ministers are always going, and who are always wanting some help. Instead of allowing themselves to be trained up to know their God and be strong, alas! it is a protracted infancy. They cannot help themselves, and therefore cannot help others. Isn't that exactly what we read in Hebrews 5:11—6:3? There we find the very same condition: those who had been so long converted and should have been teachers needed themselves to be taught the first principles of Christianity. These are people who are always wanting to be helped instead of being a help to others.

For a little child, a spiritual baby of three months old, to be carnal and not to know how to have victory over sin is, as Paul said, a thing not to be wondered at. But when a man continues year after year in the same state of always being defeated by sin, there is something radically wrong. Nothing can keep a child in protracted infancy except disease or disorder. And if we have to say continually, "I am not spiritual," then do let us say, "O God, I am carnal; I am in a diseased or disordered state, and want to be helped out of it."

The *second* mark of a carnal state is that *sin and failure prove master*. Sin has the upper hand. What proof does Paul give that those people were carnal? He first charges them and then he asks a question, "For whereas there is among you envyings, and strife, and divisions, are ye not carnal, and walk as men? For while one saith, I am of Paul; and another, I am of Apollos; are ye not carnal?" Paul in effect asks, "Isn't it obvious? You act like other men; you are not acting like heavenly renewed men who live in the power and love of the Holy Spirit. You know that God is love, that love is the great commandment, that the cross of Christ is nothing but the evidence of God's love, and that the fruit of the Holy Spirit is love." The whole of John's Gospel means *love*. But when men give way to their tempers and pride and envying and divisions; when they hear people saying sharp things about others; when a man cannot open his heart to a brother who has done him wrong and forgive him; when a woman can speak about her neighbor with contempt as, "That miserable creature," or say to another, "Oh, how I dislike that woman"—all these are the works of the carnal spirit. Every touch of unlovingness is nothing but the *flesh*. The word *carnal* is a form of the Latin word for *flesh,* and all unlovingness is nothing but the fruit or work of the flesh. The flesh is selfish and proud and unloving; therefore, every sin against love is nothing but a proof that the man is carnal.

You say, "I have tried to conquer it, but I cannot."

That is what I want to impress upon you. You cannot bear spiritual fruit while you are in the carnal state. You must have the Holy Spirit in order to love. Then the carnal will be conquered. He will give you the Spirit to walk in love.

This is true not only of the sins against love, but for all other sins. Take worldliness, which someone says has "honeycombed the church"; take the love of money; take the pursuit of business when people sacrifice everything for the increase of riches; take so much of our life, the seeking after luxury and pleasure and position. What is it all but the flesh? It gratifies the flesh; it is exactly what the world thinks desirable and delights in. If you live like the world, it is a proof that the spirit of the world which is in the flesh is in you. The carnal state is proven by the power of sin.

Someone asked me recently, "How about the lack of love of prayer?" He wanted to know how loving fellowship with God could be attained. I said, "My brother, it is impossible until you discover that it must come outside of the carnal state." The flesh cannot delight in God; that is your difficulty. It is meaningless to say or write down a resolution in your journal that "I will pray more." You cannot force it. But let the axe come to the root of the tree; cut down the carnal mind. How can you cut it down? *You* cannot, but let the Holy Spirit come with the condemnation of sin and the cross of Christ, and give the flesh over to death, and the Spirit of God will come in. Then you will learn to love prayer and love God and love your neighbor, and you will be controlled by humility and spiritual-mindedness. The carnal state is the *root* of every sin.

I come to the third point. If we want to know this carnal state thoroughly, we must take very special notice that *the carnal state can coexist with great spiritual gifts.*

Remember, there is a great difference between spiritual gifts and spiritual graces, and that is what many people do not understand. Among the Corinthians, for instance, there were many wonderful spiritual gifts. In the first chapter, Paul says, "I thank my God . . . that in everything ye are enriched by him, in all utterance, and in all knowledge." That was something wonderful to praise God for. And in the second epistle he says in effect, "You do not come behind in any gift; see that you have the gift of liberality also." And in the twelfth chapter, how he speaks about the gifts of prophecy, and of faith that could remove mountains, and of knowledge as things that they were pressing in on; but he tells them these will not profit them unless they have *love*. They delighted in the gifts, and did not concern themselves with the graces. But Paul shows them a more excellent way— to learn to love and to be humble. Love is the greatest thing of all, for love is Godlike above everything.

This is a very serious reminder that a man may be gifted with prophecy, that a man may be a faithful and successful worker in some particular sphere among the poor and needy, and yet by the sharpness of his judgment and the pride that comes into him, and by other things, he may give proof that while his spiritual gifts are wonderful, his spiritual graces are too often absent. Take care that Satan does not deceive you with the thought, "But I work for God, and God blesses me, and others look up to me, and I am the means of helping others." Beloved believer, any person who is exercising spiritual gifts, even the most earnest and successful man, must be brought to his knees before God with the thought, "Am I, even after all that God's Spirit works in me as a matter of gift, possibly giving way to the flesh in lack of humility, or love, or purity, or holiness?" God search us and try us for His name's sake.

The fourth point is that *the carnal state renders it impos-*

*sible for a man to receive spiritual truth.* This is characterized by believers who hunger for the Word, and they listen and say, "What beautiful truths, what clear doctrines, what beautiful expositions of God's Word!" and yet they receive no help from it; or they are helped for two or three weeks and the blessing passes away. What is the reason? There is an evil at the bottom; the carnal state is hindering the reception of spiritual truth.

I am afraid that in our churches we often make a tragic mistake. We preach to carnal believers what is only proper for spiritual men. These believers think it so beautiful and take it into their heads and delight in it and say, "That is grand; what a view of the truth that man can give!" Yet their lives remain unchanged; they are carnal, even after all the spiritual teaching they get. Here we need to say to God, "Lord, deliver me from taking up spiritual teaching into a carnal mind!" The only evidence that you have received a teaching is that you are lifted out of the carnal into the spiritual state. God is willing to do it. Let us plead for it and receive it.

Now comes the very important and solemn question, *Is it possible for a man to move out of the carnal into the spiritual state? And how is it possible?* I want to answer that, and to point out the steps which must be taken. I desire to speak as simply as possible, for I want to say to every honest, earnest heart that is longing to be spiritual, you can get out of the carnal state. And what is needed for that?

I think the first thing needed is that *a man must have some sight of the spiritual life and some faith in it.* Some of our hearts are so full of unbelief, without our knowing it, that we do not accept as a settled matter that we can become spiritual men. We do not believe it.

I heard an interesting story once while talking to a man of deep Christian experience. I had said to him, "Tell me about the state of the believers in England. You have worked among them and know them well." He replied, "I believe there is nothing so terrible among them as *unbelief.*" Then he told me about a young man of high promise, who was in

England working for Christ. That young man had great gifts, but my friend could not understand why, with all those gifts, he did not see more results. They spent a whole day together trying to find out what it was that was hindering the young man's ministry. It was only gradually they discovered that the root of the trouble was *unbelief*. He did not think it possible to live out the consecrated life. He was not sure that God was ready to give the blessing. The next morning they met again to discuss it more and to pray. During their discussion, the young man saw what it was to trust God for the power of a life in full surrender and received a blessing from God. Since then he had been ten times more blessed in his work than ever before. Do believe that if you are ready and willing, it is possible for God to make a spiritual man of you. Only try to get a vision of the spiritual life.

What is that vision? You know the Word speaks about two powers of life—the *flesh* and the *Spirit:* the flesh, our natural life under the power of sin; the Spirit, God's life coming to take the place of our natural life. What we need, and what the Bible tells us, is to yield our whole life, with every idea of strength or power, unto Jesus' death, to become nothing, and receive the life of Christ and of the Spirit to do all for us. Believe that it is possible.

You say, "That is so far beyond me, I can never reach it." No, you cannot, but God will send it down to you. Your reaching up is the great danger; you cannot reach it. But if you believe that God wants in a supernatural way, according to His everlasting love, to give you the power of the Holy Spirit, then God will do for you more than you can ask or think.

I believe it is possible for a man to live every day led by the Holy Spirit. I have read in God's Word that He sheds abroad His love in the heart by the Holy Spirit. I have read in God's Word that as many as are led by the Spirit, they are the children of God. I have read in God's Word that if we are born again, we are to walk by the Spirit or in the Spirit. Dear friends, it *is* possible; it is the life God calls us to and that Christ redeemed us for. After He shed His blood, He ascended to heaven to send the Spirit to His people. After He was glorified, His first work was to give the Holy Spirit. When you begin to believe in the power of Christ's blood to cleanse you and in the power of the glorified Christ to give His Spirit in your heart, you have taken the first step in the right direction.

Though you may feel ever so wretched, do hold fast to Jesus. He can fill you with the Spirit, for He has commanded you to "be filled with the Spirit."

But secondly, it is not enough that a man should have a vision of the spiritual life which is to be lived; it is also imperative *that a man should be fully convinced of his carnality*. This is a difficult and serious, but, as I say, needful lesson. There is a great difference—I ask you to notice this—between the sins of the unconverted man and the sins of the believer. As an unconverted man, you had to be convicted of sin and make confession of it. But what were you primarily convicted about? Of the grossness of sin and very much about the guilt and punishment of sin. But there was very little conviction of inward, spiritual sins. You had no knowledge of them. There was very little conviction of inward sinfulness. That does not normally come with conversion. And so, how is a man to get rid of these two things—the more hidden sins and the deep inner sinfulness? In this way: After he has become a Christian, the Holy Spirit convicts him of the carnal, fleshly life. Then the man begins to mourn over it and is ashamed of it. He cries out like Paul, "O wretched man that I am! who shall deliver me from the body of this death?" He begins to seek for help and to ask, Where am I to get deliverance? He seeks for it in many ways, by struggling and resolve; but he does not get it until he is brought to cast himself absolutely at the feet of Jesus. Do not forget that if you are to become a spiritual man, if you are to be filled with the Holy Spirit, it must come from God in heaven. God alone can do it.

How different our living and praying and preaching would be if the presence of the Holy One, who fills the universe, were revealed to us! To that end, God wants to bring us to a condition of utter brokenness. Somebody said to me, "It is dreadful that call to *die*." Yes, it is dreadful, if you had to do it in your own strength. But if you would only understand that God gave Jesus to die for us, and that God wants to join you into Jesus that you may be delivered from the accursed power of the flesh! In contrast, it is a blessing to be utterly broken down and in despair that you may learn to trust in God alone. Paul seems to say, in effect, "I had the sentence of death in myself, that I might learn not to trust in myself, but in God, who raises the dead." That is the place you must come to under conviction of your carnality—"The flesh prevails and triumphs in me, and I cannot conquer it. Have mercy, my God! God, help me!" And God *will*. Oh, become willing to bow before God in conviction and confession.

And then comes the third thing—*to believe that one can pass from the carnal to the spiritual condition in one moment of time*. People want to *grow out* of the carnal into the spiritual, and they never can. They seek more preaching and teaching, thinking they will grow out of the carnal life. The child I spoke of, though ten years old, remained as a baby of six months; he had a disease, or disorder, and needed healing. Then growth would come. Now, the carnal state is both a state of disease and disorder. The carnal believer is a babe in Christ. He is a child of God, but he cannot grow. How is the healing to come?

It must come through God, and God desires to give it this very hour.

Let me clarify that a man who becomes *a spiritual man* at this moment is not yet *a man of spiritual maturity*. I cannot expect from a young believer who has received the Holy Spirit in His fullness what I can expect from a mature Christian who has been filled with Him for twenty years. There is a great deal of growth and maturity in the spiritual life. But what I speak of when I speak of *one step* is this: You can change your place, and, instead of standing in the *carnal* life, enter the *spiritual* life in one moment.

Note the reason why the two expressions are used. In the carnal man there is something of the spiritual nature; but you know that things get their names from that which is their most prominent element. Something may be used for two or three purposes, but it will probably get its name from that which is the most prominent. It may have several characteristics, but the name will be given according to that which is the most striking. So, Paul says, in other words, to the Corinthians, "You babes in Christ are carnal; you are under the power of the flesh, giving way to temper and unloveliness, and not growing or capable of receiving spiritual truth, despite all your gifts."

The spiritual man is not a man who has reached final perfection; there still is abundant room for growth. But if you look at him, the chief mark of his nature and conduct is that he is *a man yielded to the Spirit of God*. He is not perfect, but he is a man who has taken the right position and said, "Lord God, I have given myself to be led by Your Spirit. You have received and blessed me, and the Holy Spirit now leads me." It is possible, God helping us, to leave our place on the one side and take it on the other. You may have heard the story about a sick man, seventy years of age, who was faithfully visited by a minister who talked to him about the blood of Christ. "Oh, yes," responded the man, "I know about the blood of Christ, that it can save us, and about pardon, that if God does not pardon us we cannot enter heaven." Yet the minister saw that the man was under no conviction of sin. Whatever the minister said, he said yes to, but there was no life in it, no conviction. The minister finally despaired one day and prayed, "God, help me to show this man his state." Suddenly a thought came into his mind. The floor of the man's room was strewn with sand, and the minister drew a line with his stick in the sand. On the one side he wrote the words sin, death, hell; on the other side, Christ, life, heaven. The old man asked, "What are you doing?" The minister answered: "Listen! Do you think one of these letters on the left side could get up and go over the line to the right side?" "Of course not," was the answer. Then the minster said solemnly, "Neither can a sinner who is on the left side get over to the right side. That line divides all mankind—the saved are on the right side and the unsaved are on the left. It is

Christ who must take you up from the left side and bring
you to the right side. On what side are you?" There was no
answer. The minister prayed with him, and went home praying that God would convict him. He went back the next day
and the question was, "Well, my friend, on what side are
you?" He at once answered with a sigh, "On the wrong side."
It was not long before that man welcomed the gospel and
accepted Christ.

I would like to draw a straight line and ask you who
believe and confess that God has given you His Spirit and
who know the joy of the Holy Spirit, to take your place at
the right-hand side. Then I would ask you who have felt that
you are still carnal, to come to the left side and say: "God, I
must confess that my Christian life is for the most part carnal, under the power of the flesh." Then I would plead with
you and tell you that you cannot save yourselves from the
flesh or get rid of it. You must come to Christ afresh; He can
lift you over into the new life. You belong to Christ and He
belongs to you; what you need is to cast yourselves upon Him
and He will reveal the power of His crucifixion in you, to give
you victory over the flesh. Cast yourselves, with the confession of sin, and utter helplessness, at the feet of the Lamb of
God. He can give you deliverance.

That brings me to my last thought. The first was, *a man
must see the spiritual life;* the second, *a man must be convicted of and confess his carnal state;* the third, *a man must
see that it is but one step from the one to the other;* and then,
lastly, *he must take the decisive step in the faith that Christ
is able to keep him.* Yes, it is not just a belief, it is not a
consecration in any sense of its being in our power, it is not
a surrender by the strength of our will. No. These aspects
may be present, but the great thing is that we must look to
Christ to keep us tomorrow, and the next day, and always;
we must get the life of God within us. We want a life that
will last not only until another "revival" but until death. We
want, by the grace of God, to experience the almighty indwelling and saving power of Christ and all that God can do
for us.

Oh, God is waiting; Christ is waiting; the Holy Spirit is waiting. Do you see what has been wrong and why you have been wandering in the wilderness? Do you see the good land, the land of promise, in which God is going to keep and bless you? Remember the story of Caleb and Joshua and the spies. Ten men said in effect, "We never can conquer those people." Two said, "We are able, for God has promised." Step out upon the promises of God. Listen to God's Word: "The law of the Spirit of life in Christ Jesus hath made me free from the law of sin and death." Take hold of a promise like that and claim that God will do for you through His Holy Spirit what He has offered you.

Come to Christ and disregard whether there is any new experience, any feeling, any excitement, any light, only apparent darkness. Come and stand upon the Word of God, the everlasting God. God as Father promises His Holy Spirit to every hungering child. Will He then not give it to you? How shall He not give the Holy Spirit to them that ask Him? How could He not do it? As truly as Christ was given for you on Calvary, so truly the Holy Spirit has been given for you and me. Open your hearts and be "filled with the Spirit." Come and trust the blood of Christ for the cleansing; confess the carnality of every sin and cast it into the fountain of the blood; then believe in the living Christ to bless you with the presence of His Spirit.

# 4

## *That God May Be All in All*

*"Then cometh the end, when he shall have delivered up the kingdom to God, even the Father; when he shall have put down all rule and all authority and power. For he must reign, till he hath put all enemies under his feet. The last enemy that shall be destroyed is death. For he hath put all things under his feet. But when he saith all things are put under him, it is manifest that he is excepted, which did put all things under him. And when all things shall be subdued unto him, then shall the Son also himself be subject unto him that put all things under him, that God may be all in all"* (1 Cor. 15:24–28).

What a mystery there is in this section of Scripture! We speak of the two great acts of humiliation on the part of the Lord Jesus as His descending from the throne and becoming man upon earth, a servant among men; and of His descent through the cross into the grave, the depth of humiliation under the curse. But oh! what a mystery is here—that a time is coming in the everlasting glory when the Son of Man himself shall be subjected to the Father, and shall give the kingdom into the Father's hands, and "God shall be all in all"! I cannot understand this; it passes knowledge. But I worship Christ in the glory of His subjection to the Father.

Here we learn the precious lesson: *The whole aim of*

43

*Christ's coming, the whole aim of redemption, the whole aim of Christ's work in our hearts is summed up in that one thought—"That God may be all in all."* We need to take this thought as our life motto and live it out. If we fail to see that this is Christ's object, we will never understand what He desires and will work in us. But if we realize that everything must be subordinated to God, then we have the same principle to rule our life that ruled the life of Christ. Let us meditate upon it, with the earnest prayer: "Father, we hope to be present on that wondrous day when Christ shall give up the kingdom, and when You shall be all in all. We hope to be there to see it, to experience it, and to rejoice in it throughout eternity. Help us to know something of it now. Lord God, take Your place and reveal Your glory that our hearts may bow in the dust and have but one song and one hope: *that God may be all in all.* Father, hear us, and may every heart be subjected to You, in full reality. Amen."

I said that this is what Jesus came into the world for. This is the object of redemption. But how can we understand this subject? How does it relate to me? I want to point you to two thoughts: *First, see how Christ, in His own life, realized and worked this out—"that God may be all in all." Second, see how we, in our lives, can realize it too.*

*The first thought, then, is to see how Christ realized and worked out our redemption.* Looking at Christ, I see five great steps in His life. An old author uses the very significant expression, "The Process of Jesus Christ." There is, first, *His birth,* then *His life, His death, His resurrection,* and *His ascension. In all* these steps you will see how God is *all.*

1. *His birth.* He received His life from God. It was by an act of God's omnipotence that He was born of the Virgin Mary. It was from God that He had His mission, and He continually spoke of being sent from God. Christ had His life from the Father and He always acknowledged it. This is the first thing a believer must learn from Christ. We should never view our conversion by what we may have done in repentance before God. Instead, we want to take time in God's presence

to realize that just as truly as it was the work of Almighty God to give His Son life here upon earth, so truly and really God has given His life into our hearts. We have our life from God.

2. *His life.* The life Christ had to maintain as a man was maintained in the power that God gave Him. How did He do it? He tells us: "I can do nothing of myself." He tells us that the words He spoke were the words the Father had given Him. He lived every moment of the day with this one thought: God is absolutely all, and I am a vessel in which God reveals His glory. That was the life of Christ—entire, unbroken, continuous dependence upon God; and God really was, in His life, every hour, *all in all.* That was what Christ came to show us.

Please note that this was what man was created for—to be a vessel into which God could pour His wisdom, goodness, beauty and power. That is the heritage of the believer. It is God that makes the seraphim and cherubim flames of fire. The unrestricted glory of God passes through them. They are vessels prepared by God, come from God, that they might let God's glory shine through them.

And so it was with the Son. Sin came in, the terrible sin—first, of the fallen angels, and then of man. They exalted themselves against God, would not receive the glory of God, and fell into the "outer darkness"; first the devils, and then men. Christ came to restore man, so He lived among us, day by day, and depended upon the Father for everything. Notice in His temptation in the wilderness, He would not touch a bit of bread until the Father gave it to Him. Although He was very hungry and had the power to turn a stone into bread, He would not eat until the Father sent the ministering angels. It is by this life of absolute dependence upon God that the glorified Christ will one day effect that God shall be *all in all.*

3. *His death.* He not only received His life from God, and lived it in dependence on God, but *He yielded His life to God.* He did it in obedience. What is obedience? Surrendering my will to the will of another. When a soldier bows to his gen-

eral, or a scholar to his teacher, he yields his will—and my will is my life—he gives himself to the rule and mastery and the power of another. And Christ did that. "I came not to do mine own will"; "Lo, I come to do thy will." In Gethsemane He said, "Not my will, but thine be done." On the cross He went even further by fulfilling what had been settled in Gethsemane. He yielded His life to God and thereby taught us that the only thing worth living for is *a life yielded to God, even unto death.* If you are controlling your life and spending it on yourself, even partly, you are abusing it and taking it away from God's original purpose. Learn from Christ that the beauty and purpose of having life is so that you can surrender it to God, and then have God fill it with His glory.

Jesus surrendered His life through the cross. But, we must not always look at crucifixion and death as necessary only from the side of sin. That is only half the truth—the negative side. We must look at it on the other side, the side of the Lord Jesus. Why did He yield His life to death, and what did He gain by it? He gave up His earthly life and God gave Him a heavenly life. He gave up the life of humiliation and God gave Him a life of fellowship and glory. Believer, do you desire the power and joy of a life in unbroken fellowship with God? There is only one way to secure it. Surrender your life to God. That is what Christ did. He yielded up His life to the very death into the hands of God. Do you see that in the life of Christ, God was everything, God "all in all"? Christ worked it out and proved most gloriously that God can be and must be, "all in all."

4. *His resurrection.* He was raised from the dead. What does the resurrection mean? To understand the resurrection we must first ask, what does the cross mean? In parting with His life, what does that say to us? He yielded himself in utter helplessness to wait upon God. He said, "I wait till my Father gives it to me." The grave was His humiliation. "My flesh shall rest in hope." There He waited until God the Father raised Him up in everlasting glory. The time of Jesus in the grave was a very short time—only three days; yet it teaches us the lesson of fully surrendering our life into God's hands,

to let God do all in us, to let God be "all in all." Surrender yourself in utter dependence upon God. Lose everything and God will raise you up in glory. Christ could never have ascended to sit upon the throne, nor could have accomplished His work of preparing the kingdom that He could give to the Father, if He had not begun by surrendering himself and letting God do all.

5. *His ascension.* This same principle holds true for His ascension and entering into glory.

Well, then, the five steps we have been considering are these: Christ received His life from God; He lived it in dependence upon God; He yielded it in death to God; He received it in the resurrection from God; and He ascended to God, and was glorified in it with God forever.

Remember that the throne in heaven is not the throne of the Lamb of God alone; it is the throne of God and the Lamb. Jesus went to share the throne with the Father; the Father was always the first and Jesus second. Even on the throne of heaven our glorified Lord Jesus honors the Father as Father. It is the deep mystery of the blessed subordination of the Son to the Father. We should meditate upon it until our souls are full of this blessed truth: Even Jesus Christ lives in subordination to the Father and because He sits in this spirit on the throne of glory, He will one day deliver the kingdom to the Father.

Let us consider this—which I said was my *first* great thought—that the Lord Jesus came to remove the terrible curse that sin had wrought, the terrible ruin that had come by man's pride and self-exaltation; and He came to live out, during thirty-three years, *that God must be all in all.*

And let me ask, in passing, Did God disappoint Him? I tell you, no. God lifted Him to the throne of the everlasting glory and to equality on the throne with himself, because He had humbled himself to honor His God. Here we learn that the place of God's blessing is in humility and dependence upon Him.

Now we come to the *second* thought: *Are we called to live as Christ lived, that God may be all in all?* Is Christ under any greater obligation to let God be all in all than us? Most people think so, but the Bible does not. The obligation should be greater on us, for He is the Son of the Father and God with God; but we are creatures of the dust. The sole purpose for our existence is that God may be "all in all," in us and to us. Have we understood that, have we expected it, have we sought for it, and have we ever learned to say with Christ: It is worth yielding everything that God may have His place and be "all in all"?

*But how can we attain to such a life?* All our teaching about consecration is useless unless its result is that God is our *all*. What do we mean by the phrase "surrendering ourselves as a living sacrifice"? This is not possible for us unless God truly is *all* in our life. Why is there so much complaining about weakness, failure, lost blessing, of walking in the dark? It can only be that God has not been given His rightful place in our lives. I am not addressing carnal believers now; I say this of the best among us. God does not get His place. I ask you to pray with your whole heart that God would take His place in your life and that the inconceivable majesty of God may be so revealed that you shall sink as atoms in the dust, and say: "God, be all, take all, and have all." God help us to do so.

*The second thought is, what are the steps by which we can be brought, in some measure, to live like Christ every day, so that God may be "all in all"?*

First of all, *take time and trouble to give God His place.* Study your God, meditate more upon your God than you have done, and try to discover the place that God desires in your life. Do not be content with the vague conception that there is the throne in the heavens where God reigns. Remember, God is not only an outward being, so to speak. There is a locality and a throne where the glory of God is especially revealed; but God has an inward being. He is revealed even in nature, and how much more in the hearts of believers! To get some conception of what the place of God is, words do not suffice. I can only say this: God is the fountain of all life.

Every bit of life in the universe is the work of God. If you really give God His place, then you will receive the humbling conviction that there is nothing but what has come from God; that God fills all things. The Bible says He works all in all, and so you will begin to say: If God is everywhere and revealed in everything, I should see Him in nature, in providence, and in everything; I should always be seeing my God. When the believer sees God everywhere, he begins to give God His place. He cannot rise in the morning without giving God His place and saying: "Lord God, You glorious Being, You are 'all in all.' " He begins to say to his fellow believers: My brothers, I am afraid that in our prayer meetings we do not let God take His place. We pray because we believe in God and know something about God; but how little we comprehend the everlasting God! In our prayer meetings the everlasting God of heaven is present! If He gets His place He will take charge of the meetings, will give blessing, and will work by His mighty power.

Oh, just to think of it! Take our minister, for instance. He guides our meeting, he calls on one to pray and another to speak; he tells us what to sing and orders what is to be done. He has a little kingdom in this tent, he manages it, and you are grateful for it. But where is God in all of this? Yes, we thank God for our ministers and leaders and for every earthly gift. But oh, that we might each learn to understand that in the church, in the prayer meeting, in our private devotions, we must give time to let our God take His place.

Will God do it? God is waiting to do it. *God longs to do it.* Just as one takes the place of the master or mistress in your house and sits at the head of the table, orders the servant, and manages everything, so God is willing in my heart and in yours to take the place of Master and of God. Brethren, have we given this glorious God the place He rightfully deserves? God forgive us if *we* have taken the place that Christ's redemption has given Him, and the place that Christ wants to give Him in us. Let us say: God shall have His place.

I might press still further in this connection of the church.

Has God His place there? Alas! Very seldom. May God humble us and stir in us an unquenchable longing, "that God may be all in all."

That is my first lesson: *Give God His place*; but take the time and trouble to do it. Take heed and be quiet. The prophet says: "Be silent all flesh before the Lord." Let the flesh be kept down. Wait, and give God time to reveal himself.

The second answer to the question, *How am I* to attain this, "That God may be all in all," and to work it out and prove it? is, *accept God's will in everything*.

Where do I find God's will? I find God's will in His Word. I have often heard people say, "I believe that every word within these two covers has come from God"; and I have sometimes heard it said, "I want to believe every promise between these two covers"; but I have seldom heard it said, "I accept every commandment within these two covers." But let us say it. If you like, write in the front page of your Bible: "Every promise of God in this book I intend to believe, every command of God in this book I purpose to obey." That is one step in the way to let God be "all in all." Surrender your life to be the embodiment and expression and incarnation of the will of God.

The second lesson is, *accept the will of God, not only in the Bible, but also in providence*. I find thousands of believers who have never learned that lesson. Do you know what that means? When Joseph's brethren sold him, he accepted God's hand in that and despite the injustices that followed we read that "God was with him." He was not parted from God when he had to part from his home. I read of David that when Shimei cursed him, he said, in effect, that he met God there in that cursing from Shimei, because God allowed it. When Judas came to kiss Christ and betray Him, when the soldiers bound Him, when Peter denied Him, when Caiaphas condemned Him, when Pilate gave Him over, Christ saw God in everything. Therefore Christ could drink the cup, for He saw the hand of the Father holding it.

Let us learn in every trial and trouble, great and little, to see God at once. Meet your God there, and let God be "all

in all." Not a hair of your head can fall without the will of
your Father. Meet the will of your Father in every trial, in
the deepest trial and the heaviest; the Son of God walks
there. And in the smallest trials—the person who irritates
you, the child who hinders you, the friend who may have
hurt you, the enemy who has reproached you, who has spoken evil of you and robbed you of your good name, the difficulty that worries you—oh! why not say: It is God who comes
to me in every difficulty. I will meet Him, and honor Him,
and give myself to Him. He will keep me!

There are two great privileges in meeting God in a difficulty and knowing Him. The first is that even though the
difficulty may have come through my own fault, if I confess
it, then I can say: God has allowed me to come into this
situation, to come into this difficulty in order to teach me a
lesson. In this situation God desires me to glorify Him. And
if God brings you into a difficulty by an act of your own, then
you can count upon it that God will give you the grace to be
humble and patient and to be perfected through the suffering
and chastisement, that in everything He may take His place.
You will be able to look to Him with absolute confidence
when you can say, "You have brought me here, and not man,
and You alone can take me out of it." Oh! if you would only
allow God to be "all in all" in every providence, what a blessed
life you would be living! Nothing can separate you from the
love of God in Christ Jesus. You have a wonderful place
provided for you in His love. Learn to take this as the key
out of every difficulty—*God is all in all.* And in prayer, day
by day, make it your earnest supplication that God may be
all.

The third lesson is, *trust His almighty power.* Trust Him
every day. If we could only begin to understand that the
whole of our Christian life is to be the work of God himself.
Paul speaks of it so often. "It is God that worketh in you both
to will and to do." The will and the desire to obey—that is
God's work in you, and that is only half of it. But He will
work *to do,* as well as *to will,* if you will acknowledge Him
in your life as *all.* In Hebrews we read: "The God of peace

. . . make you perfect in every good work to do his will, working in you that which is well-pleasing in his sight, through Jesus Christ." Just as a watchmaker makes a watch—cuts it, cleans it, polishes it, and has put in every little wheel and every little spring—so the living God is actually and actively engaged in the work of perfecting your life every moment. God is willing to work in your life every moment, but why does He not work more powerfully? Simply because you do not yield to His power, you do not fully give Him His place, you do not wait upon Him to do it. Tell Him: "My God, here I am now. I give You Your place in my life."

Supppose that when a painter came into his studio to paint an unfinished picture, the canvas had moved to some other part of the room. Until moved back, the painter could not paint. But suppose the canvas began to say: I will be still; come and do your work and paint your beautiful picture. Then the painter would come and do it. And if you say to God "You are the mighty Workman, the wondrous Artist. I am still. Here I am. I trust Your power and believe You," then He will work wonders in you. God never works anything but wonders. That is His nature, even in what we call the laws of nature. Take the simplest thing, a blade of grass, or a little worm, or a flower; what wonders men of science tell us about them. And will not God work wonders in my heart and yours? He will. And why doesn't He do it more? Because we do not allow Him. Learn to give Him His place, to accept His will, and then to trust His mighty work.

> In Thy strength I lay me down,
>     Clay within the Potter's hands,
> Molded by Thy gentle will,
>     Mightier than all commands:
> Moved and shaped by Thee alone,
> Now and evermore Thine own.

Is that true of you? God is willing to mold you as really as the potter molds his clay. He will do it. Let us believe and trust His mighty power to do things above what we could ask or think. *God is waiting to do for you more than you can even conceive.* Every yearning of your heart, every message that you have heard, of which you have said, "I wish I had that"; every prayer you have sent up—just believe that God is willing to work it all in you and that He is waiting to do it. In every difficulty and every circumstance, God is there to work in you. Trust Him and honor Him and let Him be "all in all."

And then, once again, if you would honor God, *sacrifice everything for His kingdom and glory*. If God is to be all in all, we must not come with the idea that I must be happy, and I must be holy, and I must have God's approval. No. The root principle of Christ's life was self-sacrifice to God for man. That is what He came for and it is a principle that every believer carries within him as unquenchable; but, alas! it can be smothered. Remember that your God longs to rule the world, and your Christ is upon the throne, desiring to lead you as His soldiers and bless you with victory upon victory. Have you yielded yourself to God's glory? Alas, alas! The soldier upon earth says: Anything for my king and country, anything when my general leads me on to victory. I yield my home life and its comforts; I yield my life. Are earthly kings to have such devotion, and you and I merely *talk* about the glory of God and His being "all in all"? Can we afford to *talk* when we are called to help prepare the kingdom for Christ to give up to the Father, and when Christ tells us He is waiting for our help and depending upon it?

Instead, let us determine that God shall be "all in all"; I will sacrifice everything for Him. May God help us to make a fresh consecration of our whole being for the furtherance of Christ's kingdom. And whether it be in mission work far away or in Christian work near to home, whether we do know how to work for Christ or not, let us yield ourselves as a willing sacrifice to be used for the glory of God.

Let this be your motto and watchword: Sacrifice everything and anything for the glory of your God. And if you do not know what to sacrifice, ask Him. Be honest, be earnest, be simple, be childlike, and say: "Lord, every penny I have and every comfort I enjoy is Yours. If You need it for Your kingdom, I offer it to You." Let me ask you this: In eternity will anyone be sorry for having made himself poor in order to help bring about that majestic spectacle of the Son saying, "It is finished," and giving the kingdom to the Father, "that God may be all in all"? Do you hope to be there? Do you hope to have a share in the glory of that majestic scene? Are you unwilling to say: "Anything that I can do for that glory, Lord, here I am?" Surrender yourself to Him.

In conclusion, there is one last thought, *Wait on God.*

It is one thing to speak and to think about God. But to know God in His glory within our souls, that is another thing. It is necessary to meditate and study, and try to form a right conception of the place God should occupy in your life. But that is not enough. You must do something else. I said: Yield yourselves to the will of God, prove the power of God, and seek the glory of God throughout the earth. But the most important step is to wait upon God.

And why must we do that? Because it is only God who can reveal himself. Remember that when God came to Adam, or Noah, or Abraham, or Moses, it was God who met them and showed himself in some form to them. That was under the old dispensation. And it still depends on the good pleasure of God to reveal himself. This is not an arbitrary good pleasure. No. It all depends upon whether He has found a heart hungering for Him. Oh, that God would awaken that hunger and teach us to cry like David, "My soul thirsteth for God!" Wait upon God. Make that an increasing priority in your life. Perhaps we need to learn a lesson on quietness from the Quakers. In your private devotions learn the lesson of keeping silence before God with this one prayer, "Lord God, reveal yourself in the depths of my heart." And though you do not expect a vision, though you do not receive a manifestation—that is not what *should* be sought; it is that the soul should open itself to God and wait upon Him that He may come in. "Verily, thou art a God that hidest thyself." You cannot always see Him, but He will come in and take possession of you, revealing himself and working mightily in you, if you are hungering for Him. Wait upon God. In your prayer meetings, let that be the first thing. It is to the detriment of both our private devotions and our prayer meetings that we begin to immediately pray as if all was right. "Oh yes," we say, "God will do it"; and yet we fail to let our souls worship in holy awe and reverence and childlike trust. We do not take time to say: "Father, let it please You to come near and to meet me."

The responsibility resting upon us is tremendous. Many of us sense we have received a secret on living the Christian life which other believers do not know. We do not judge, but we confess that God has taught us something wonderful. Let us confess it boldly. But then, if that is true, we must come still nearer to God and have more of God in order to teach others how they can find God. You cannot find God without waiting upon Him. "Wait, I say, on the Lord."

If we take the steps given here, God will be our all in all. Then we will be prepared for taking our place in that glorious company who shall be present at that sublime, magnificent scene when Christ shall give up the kingdom to the Father— *"that God may be all in all."*

# 5

## *Set Apart to the Holy Spirit*

*"Now there were in the church that was at Antioch certain prophets and teachers; as Barnabas, and Simeon that was called Niger, and Lucius of Cyrene, and Manaen ... and Saul. As they ministered to the Lord, and fasted, the Holy Ghost said, Separate me Barnabas and Saul for the work whereunto I have called them. And when they had fasted and prayed, and laid their hands on them, they sent them away. So they, being sent forth by the Holy Ghost, departed unto Seleucia"* (Acts 13:1–4).

Our purpose has been to discover the will of our God concerning His work and to seek Him for the accompanying power. The story of our text includes some precious thoughts to guide us concerning this. The great lesson of the verses is this: *The Holy Spirit is the director of the work of God upon the earth.* If we are to work for God, and if God is to bless our work, we must stand in a right relation to the Holy Spirit. He must daily receive the place of honor that belongs to Him, so that in all our work and in all our private inner life, the Holy Spirit shall always have the first place. Let me point out some of the precious thoughts our passage suggests.

First of all, we see that *God has His own plans ragarding His kingdom.* His church at Antioch had been established.

God had certain plans and intentions regarding Asia and Europe and He made them known to His servants. Our great Commander organizes the campaign, but His generals and officers do not always know the great plans. They often receive sealed orders and have to wait on Him for what He gives them as orders. God in heaven has specific plans; we cannot doubt it. God in heaven has wishes and a will in regard to the work that should be done and to the way in which it has to be done. Blessed is the man who gets into God's secrets and works under God.

Some years ago at Wellington, we opened a Mission Institute—which was considered a fine large building. At our opening services the Principal said something I have never forgotten. He remarked: "Last year we gathered here to lay the foundation stone, and what was there then to be seen? Nothing but rubbish, stones, bricks, and the ruins of an old building that had been pulled down. There we laid the foundation stone and very few knew what the building would be like. No one knew it perfectly in every detail except one man, the architect. In his mind it was all clear, and as the contractor and the mason and the carpenter came to their work, they took their orders from him. As the workers were obedient to orders, the structure rose and this beautiful building has been completed. And just so," he added, "this building that we opened today is but laying the foundation of a work of which only God knows what it is to become." But God has His workers and His plans clearly mapped out; our position is to wait until God communicates to us as much of His will required for each moment.

We are simply to be faithful in obedience, carrying out His orders. God has a plan for His Church upon earth. Unfortunately, we too often make our own plan and think that we know what should be done. We first ask God to bless our feeble efforts instead of absolutely refusing to go unless God goes before us. God has planned for the work and the extension of His kingdom. The Holy Spirit has this work as His responsibility. "The work whereunto *I* have called them." The work to be done by the Church is Holy Spirit work. May

God therefore help us all to be afraid of touching "the ark of God" except as we are led by the Holy Spirit.

Then the second thought. *God is willing and able to reveal to His servants what His will is.* Yes, communications still come down from heaven. What the Holy Spirit said to the church in Antioch He will speak to His Church and His people today. He has often done it. He has come to individual men and by His divine teaching has led them out into fields of labor that others could not at first understand or approve, into ways and methods that did not recommend themselves to the majority. But the Holy Spirit is still teaching His people. Thank God, in both our missionary societies and in our home missions, in a thousand forms of work, the guiding of the Holy Spirit is known, but we are all ready, I think, to confess *too little* known. We have not learned to wait upon Him enough to fully know His will.

Do not ask God only for power. Many believers have their own plan of working, but God must send the power. They work in their own will and think that God must give the grace—this is why God so often gives so little grace and so little success. Let us take our place before God and say: "What is done in the will of God, the strength of God will not be withheld from; what is done in the will of God must have the mighty blessing of God." And so let our first desire be to have the will of God revealed.

If you ask whether it is easy to receive these communications from heaven, I can give you the answer. It is easy to those who are in right fellowship with heaven and who understand the art of waiting upon God. How often have we asked how we can know the will of God. And people want, when they are perplexed, to pray very earnestly that God should answer them at once. But God can reveal His will only to a heart that is humble and tender and quiet. God can reveal His will in perplexities and special difficulties only to a heart that has learned to obey and honor Him loyally in little things and in daily life.

That brings me to the third thought, *the disposition to*

*which the Spirit reveals God's will.* What do we read here?
There were a number of men ministering to the Lord and
fasting when the Holy Spirit came and spoke to them. Some
people understand this passage to the same degree as they
would in reference to a missionary committee of our day. Our
attention is brought to an open field and we decide we are
going to start a work there. We have virtually settled that,
then we pray about it. But our position is out of line. I doubt
whether any of them had considered Europe, for later on
even Paul tried to go back into Asia until the night vision
called him by the will of God. Look at those men. God had
done wonders, had extended the Church to Antioch, and had
given rich and large blessing. Here these men are ministering to the Lord, serving Him with prayer and fasting. What
a deep conviction they have—it must all come direct from
heaven. We are in fellowship with the risen Lord; out of this
close union with Him He will let us know what He wants.
And there they were, quiet and waiting, glad and joyful, but
deeply humbled. O Lord, they seem to say, we are Your servants and in fasting and prayer we wait upon You. What is
Your will for us?

Was it not the same with Peter? He was on the housetop,
fasting and praying, and not expecting the vision and command to go to Caesarea. He was ignorant of what his work
might be. May God grant that this may become our position—our hearts entirely surrendered to the Lord Jesus, our
hearts separated from the world and even from ordinary religious exercises, and giving ourselves in intense prayer to
look to our Lord—it is in such hearts that the heavenly will
of God will be made manifest.

Notice that the word "fasting" occurs a second time (Acts
13:3): "They fasted and prayed." When you pray, you love to
go into a private place, according to the command of Jesus,
and shut the door. You shut out business, company, pleasure
and anything that can distract your desire to be alone with
God. Yet, the material world even follows you there. You
must eat. These men desired to shut themselves out from the
influences of the material and the visible, so they fasted. In

the intensity of their souls, they gave expression to their letting go of everything on earth in their fasting before God. Oh, may God give us that intensity of desire, that separation from everything, because we desire to wait upon Him that the Holy Spirit may reveal to us His blessed will.

The fourth thought is, *what has the Holy Spirit revealed concerning the will of God?* It is contained in this: *being set apart to the Holy Spirit*. That is the keynote of the message from heaven. "Separate me Barnabas and Saul for the work whereunto I have called them." In effect, God said that this is mine and I care for it, I have chosen these men and called them, and I want you who represent the Church of Christ upon earth to set them apart to me.

Look at this heavenly message in its twofold aspect. The men were to be *set apart* to the Holy Spirit, and *the Church was to do this separating work*. The Holy Spirit could trust these men to do it in a right spirit. They were abiding in fellowship with the Father and were under the leadership of the Holy Spirit. Because these were the men the Holy Spirit had prepared, He could say of them, "Let them be separated to me."

This brings us to the very root, to the very life of our need as workers. The question asked is, What is necessary for the power of God to rest upon us, that the blessing of God should be poured out more abundantly among the lost and perishing sinners among whom we labor? The answer from heaven is, I want men separated to the Holy Spirit. What does this imply? Christ said, when He spoke about the Holy Spirit, "The world cannot receive him." Paul said, "We have received not the spirit of the world, but the Spirit that is of God." That is the great need in every worker—the spirit of the world being displaced by the incoming Spirit of God who takes possession of the inner life and of the whole being.

No doubt many of us often cry to God for the Holy Spirit to come upon us as a Spirit of power for our work, and when we feel that measure of power we thank God for it. But God desires something more, something higher. God desires us to seek for the Holy Spirit as a Spirit of power in our own heart and life to conquer self and cast out sin and to work the blessed and beautiful image of Jesus into us.

There is a difference between the power of the Spirit as a gift and the power of the Spirit for the grace of a holy life. A man may often have a measure of the power of the Spirit, but if He does not rule the heart as the Spirit of grace and of holiness, the defect will be manifest in his work. The man may have been effective in evangelism, but he will never help people onto a higher standard of spiritual life. When he dies, a great deal of his work may pass away too. But a man who is separated to the Holy Spirit is a man who says: "Father, let the Holy Spirit have full dominion over me—in my home, in my disposition, and in every word of my tongue, in every thought of my heart, in every feeling toward others; let the Holy Spirit have entire possession." Has that been the desire and the covenant of your heart with your God— to be a man or a woman separated and yielded to the Holy Spirit? Listen to the voice of heaven again. "Separate me," said the Holy Spirit. Yes, set apart to the Holy Spirit. May God grant that the Word may enter into the very depths of our being to search us, and if God discovers to us that the self-life, self-will, self-exaltation are there, let us humble ourselves before Him. Let us fully come out from the world.

It is necessary for us to take time to humble ourselves before God and to ask Him to humble us under His mighty hand. Man, woman, brother, sister, you are a worker set apart to the Holy Spirit. Is that true? Has that been your longing desire? Has that been your surrender? Has that been what you have expected through faith in the power of our risen and almighty Lord Jesus? If not, here is the call of faith and the key of blessing: set apart to the Holy Spirit. May God write the word in our hearts!

I said the Holy Spirit spoke to that church as a church capable of doing that work. The Holy Spirit trusted them. God grant that our churches, our missionary societies, our Sunday schools, that all our directors and councils and committees may be men and women who are equipped for the

task of *separating workers to the Holy Spirit*. We can ask God
that as Christian workers we should be enabled to separate
each other to the Holy Spirit. May God make us worthy of
doing the work for each other.

Then comes my fifth thought: *This holy partnership with
the Holy Spirit in His work becomes a matter of consciousness
and of action*. These men, what did they do? They set apart
Paul and Barnabas, and then it is written of the two that
they, being sent forth by the Holy Spirit, went down to Seleucia. Oh, what fellowship! The Holy Spirit in heaven doing
part of the work, man on earth doing the other part. After
the ordination of the men upon earth, it is written in God's
inspired Word that they were sent forth by the Holy Spirit.

And see how this partnership calls to new prayer and
fasting. They had been fasting and ministering to the Lord
for a certain time, perhaps days; the Holy Spirit gave the
directions for the work and immediately they came together
for more prayer and fasting. That is the spirit in which they
obeyed the command of their Lord. It teaches us that it is
not only in the beginning of our Christian work, but all along,
that we need to have our strength in prayer. If there is one
thought with regard to the Church which comes to me with
overwhelming sorrow; if there is one thought in regard to
my own life of which I am ashamed; if there is one thought
that I feel the Church has not accepted nor grasped; if there
is one thought which makes me pray, "Oh, teach us by Your
grace new things"—*it is the wonderful power that prayer is
meant to have in the kingdom*. We have so little availed ourselves of it!

You may have read the expression of Christian in Bun-
yan's great work, when he found he had the key in his breast
that would unlock the dungeon. We have this key that can
unlock the dungeon around us and of heathendom. But, oh,
*we are far more occupied with our work than we are in prayer.
We believe more in speaking to men than we believe in speaking to God*. Learn from these men that the work which the
Holy Spirit commands must call us to new fasting and prayer,

to new separation from the spirit and the pleasures of the world, to new consecration to God and to His fellowship. Those men yielded themselves to fasting and prayer, and if in all our ordinary Christian work there were more prayer, there would be more blessing in our own inner life. If we were convinced that our only strength is found in abiding every minute with Christ, every minute allowing God to work in us—if that were our spirit, wouldn't our lives be holier? Wouldn't they be more abundantly fruitful?

There are few warnings in God's Word more solemn than that which we find in Galatians three, where Paul asked, "Having begun in the Spirit, are ye now made perfect by the flesh?" Do you understand what that means? A terrible danger in Christian work, just as in a Christian life that is begun with much prayer and in the Holy Spirit, is that it may gradually swerve off onto the lines of the flesh; the word comes, "Having begun in the Spirit, are ye now made perfect by the flesh?" In our beginning perplexity and helplessness we prayed much to God; God answered and blessed; our organization became perfected and our group of workers was enlarged; but gradually the organization and the work and the rush so got possession of us that the power of the Spirit was nearly lost completely. Oh, I pray you, note it well! It was with new prayer and fasting, with more prayer and fasting, that this company of disciples carried out the command of the Holy Spirit. "My soul, wait thou only upon God." That is our highest amd most important work. The Holy Spirit comes in answer to believing prayer.

You remember that when the exalted Jesus had ascended to the throne, for ten days the footstool of the throne was the place where His waiting disciples cried to Him. And that is the law of the kingdom—the King upon the throne, the servants upon the footstool. May God find us there unceasingly.

Then comes the last thought, *the wonderful blessing that comes when the Holy Spirit is allowed to direct the work and when it is carried on in obedience to Him!* You know the story of the mission on which Barnabas and Saul were sent out.

You know what power there was with them. The Holy Spirit sent them and they went on from place to place with great blessing. The Holy Spirit was their leader further on. You remember that the Spirit hindered Paul from going again into Asia and instead led him into Europe. Oh, the blessing that rested upon that little company of men and upon their ministry!

The secret is to believe that God has a blessing for us. The Holy Spirit, into whose hands God has put the work, has been called "the executive of the Holy Trinity." The Holy Spirit has not only the power but is the Spirit of love. He is brooding over this dark world and every sphere of work within it. He is willing to bless. Why is there not more blessing? There can only be one answer. We have not honored the Holy Spirit as we should. Can anyone lift up the hand and say it is not true? Is not every thoughtful heart ready to cry, "God, forgive me that I have not honored the Holy Spirit as I have done, that I have grieved Him, that I have allowed self and the flesh and my own will to work where the Holy Spirit should have been honored? May God forgive me that I have allowed self and the flesh and the will to actually have the place that God wanted the Holy Spirit to have." Oh, the sin is greater than we know! No wonder there is so much feebleness and failure in the Church!

# 6

## *Peter's Repentance*

*"And the Lord turned, and looked upon Peter. And Peter remembered the word of the Lord, how he had said unto him, Before the cock crow, thou shalt deny me thrice. And Peter went out and wept bitterly"* (Luke 22:61, 62).

This was the turning point in the history of Peter. Christ had said to him, "Thou canst not follow me now." Peter was not able to follow Christ because he had not been brought to an end of himself; he did not know himself and therefore could not follow Christ. But when he went out and wept bitterly, then the great change came. Christ previously said to him, "When thou art converted, strengthen thy brethren." Here is the point where Peter was converted from self to Christ.

I thank God for the story of Peter. I do not know a man in the Bible who gives us greater comfort. When we look at his character, so full of failures, and at what Christ made him by the power of the Holy Spirit, there is hope for each of us. But remember, before Christ could fill Peter with the Holy Spirit and make a new man of him, Peter had to go out and weep bitterly; he had to be humbled. To understand this, I think there are four points that we must look at. First, let us look at *Peter the devoted disciple of Jesus;* second, *as he lived the life of self;* third, *in his repentance;* and, fourth, *deliverance from self.*

First, *Peter the devoted disciple of Jesus.* Christ called Peter to forsake his nets and follow Him. Peter did it at once and afterward could truthfully say to the Lord, "We have forsaken all, and followed thee." Peter was a man of *entire surrender;* he surrendered all to follow Jesus. Peter was also a man of *true obedience.* You remember that Christ said to him, "Launch out into the deep, and let down the net." Peter the fisherman knew there were no fish there; they had been toiling all night and had caught nothing. But he said, "At thy word I will let down the net." He submitted to the word of Jesus. Further, he was a man of *great faith.* When he saw Christ walking on the sea, he said, "Lord, if it be thou, bid me come unto thee"; and at the voice of Christ he stepped out of the boat and walked upon the water. Peter was also a man of *spiritual insight.* When Christ asked the disciples, "Whom do ye say that I am?" Peter was able to answer, "Thou art the Christ, the Son of the living God." And Christ said, "Blessed art thou, Simon Barjona; for flesh and blood hath not revealed it unto thee, but my Father which is in heaven." Christ spoke of him as the *rock* man and of his having the keys of the kingdom. Peter was a splendid man, a devoted disciple of Jesus. And yet how much there was lacking in Peter!

Second, *Peter lived the life of self—pleasing self, trusting self, and seeking the honor of self.* Just after Christ had said to Peter, "Flesh and blood hath not revealed it unto thee, but my Father which is in heaven," Christ began to speak about His sufferings and Peter dared to say, "Be it far from thee, Lord; this shall not be unto thee." Then Christ had to say, "Get thee behind me, Satan; for thou savourest not the things that be of God, but those that be of men." There was Peter in his self-will, trusting his own wisdom, and actually forbidding Christ to go and die. What prompted this? Peter trusted himself and his own thoughts about divine things.

We see later on, more than once, that when the disciples were questioning among themselves who should be the greatest, Peter was one of them. He thought he had a right to the very first place. He sought his own honor even above the others. It was the life of self strong in Peter.

When Christ had spoken to him about His sufferings and said, "Get thee behind me, Satan," He followed it up by saying, "If any man will come after me, let him deny himself, and take up his cross, and follow me." No man can follow Him unless he does that. Self must be utterly denied. What does that mean? When Peter denied Christ, we read that three times he said, "I do not know the man." In other words, "I have nothing to do with Him; He and I are not friends; I deny having any connection with Him." Christ told Peter that he must deny self. Self must be ignored and its every claim rejected. That is the root of true discipleship; but Peter did not understand it and could not obey it. Consequently, when the last night came Christ said to him, "Before the cock crow twice thou shalt deny me thrice." But with what self-confidence Peter said, "Though all should forsake thee, yet will not I. I am ready to go with thee to prison and to death." Peter truly meant it and really intended to do it; but Peter did not know himself.

Perhaps we do not know ourselves so well either. Do we give place to our own self-life? What have we done with the flesh that is entirely under the power of sin? Deliverance from that is what we need. Peter did not understand this, and therefore in self-confidence he went forth and denied his Lord.

Notice how Christ used that word *deny* twice. He said to Peter the first time, *Deny self;* He said to Peter the second time, *Thou wilt deny me.* It is either one or the other. There is no alternative; we must either deny self or deny Christ. There are two great powers fighting each other—the self-life in the power of sin, and Christ in the power of God. One of these must rule within us.

Third, *Peter's repentance.* Peter denied the Lord three

times before the Lord looked upon him; that look of Jesus broke the heart of Peter. That look exposed the terrible sin that he had committed, the terrible failure that had come, the depth into which he had fallen, and "Peter went out and wept bitterly."

Oh! who can tell what that repentance must have been? During the following hours of that night and the next day, when he saw Christ crucified and buried, and the next day, the Sabbath—oh, in what hopeless despair and shame he must have spent that day! "My Lord is gone, my hope is gone, and I denied my Lord. After that life of love, after that blessed fellowship of three years, I denied my Lord. God have mercy upon me!" I do not think it is possible to imagine into what depths of humiliation Peter sank. But that was the turning point and the change; on the first day of the week Christ was seen by Peter and in the evening He met him with the others. Later on at the Lake of Galilee He asked him, "Lovest thou me?" until Peter was saddened by the thought that the Lord reminded him of having denied Him. He said in sorrow, but in uprightness, "Lord, thou knowest all things; thou knowest that I love thee."

Fourth, *Peter's deliverance from self.* You know Christ took him with the others to the footstool of the throne and told him to wait there; on the Day of Pentecost the Holy Spirit came and Peter was a changed man. We usually only see the change in Peter in that boldness and power, that insight into the Scriptures, and that blessing with which he preached that day. Thank God for that. But there was something deeper and better for Peter. Peter's whole nature was changed.

If you want to see that, read the First Epistle of Peter. You know where Peter's failings lay. When he said to Christ, in effect, "You must never suffer; it cannot be"—it showed he had not understood what it was to pass through death into life. Christ said, "Deny thyself," and in spite of that Peter denied his Lord. When Christ warned him, "Thou shalt deny me," and he insisted that he never would, Peter showed how little he understood himself. But when I read his epistle and hear him say, "If ye be reproached for the name of Christ, happy are ye; for the spirit of glory and of God resteth upon you," then I know that is not the old Peter but the very Spirit of Christ breathing and speaking within him. I read how he says, "Hereunto ye are called to suffer, even as Christ suffered." I understand what a change had come over Peter. Instead of denying Christ, he found joy and pleasure in having self denied and crucified and given up to the death. And therefore it is in Acts we read that when he was called before the Council he could boldly say, "We must obey God rather than men"; he could return with the other disciples and rejoice that they were counted worthy to suffer for Christ's name. Dear friends, I beseech you, look at Peter utterly changed—the self-pleasing, the self-trusting, the self-seeking Peter filled with the Spirit and life of Jesus. Christ had done it for him by the Holy Spirit.

So what is my object in having briefly pointed to the story of Peter? That story must be the history of every worker who really is to be used by God. That story has been, praise God, the history of more than one worker. Peter's story is a prophecy of what each of us can receive from God in heaven. We must not only pray for God's work and talk about it; not only pray for an outpouring of the Spirit of love and that God would bind us together in the power of love; but we must come together especially for God to deal with every individual life. For it is when the individual workers are blessed that the work will prosper and the body will be in health and strength.

Now let us briefly observe the lessons taught here.

The first lesson is this: *It is possible to be a very earnest, godly, devoted, and to some extent, successful worker in whom the power of the flesh is yet very strong.*

That is a very solemn truth, and God only knows the depth of it in our service. Peter, before he denied Christ, had cast out demons and had healed the sick. There are many who have been serving God with success and want to praise Him for the blessing; and yet, just like Peter, the flesh has freedom and power. What we must realize is that because there is so much self-life in us, the power of God cannot work in us as mightily as He desires. Do you realize that God is longing to double His blessing, to give tenfold blessing through us? But there is something hindering Him, and that something is nothing but the self-life. We talk about the pride of Peter, the impulsiveness of Peter, the self-confidence of Peter. It's all rooted in that one word *self*. When Christ had said, "Deny self," Peter never understood and never obeyed; and every failure came out of that.

And so I say there may be children of God, servants of God—ministers, leaders of large works, people of power and position and talent, or even the simple and humble workers—working earnestly for God, in whom the self-life prevails. What a solemn thought and what an urgent plea for us to cry, "Lord, expose this that none of us may be living the self-life!" It has happened to many a man who has worked for twenty years, perhaps occupied a prominent position, that God has revealed the inner life, and he has become utterly ashamed and fallen down broken before God. Oh, the bitter shame and sorrow and pain and agony that comes to him until he finds at last that there is deliverance! Peter went out and wept bitterly, and there may be the same need for weeping in our lives.

The second lesson is: *It is the work of our blessed Lord Jesus to discover the power of self.*

How was it that Peter, the carnal Peter, self-willed Peter, Peter with the strong self-love, ever became a man of Pentecost and the writer of his epistle? It was because Christ had him as His disciple, Christ watched over him, Christ taught and blessed him. The warnings that Christ had given him were part of the training; and, last of all, there came that look of love. In His suffering Christ did not forget him, but turned around and looked upon him, and "Peter went out and wept bitterly." The Christ who led Peter to Pentecost is among us today and is waiting to take charge of every heart that is willing to surrender to Him.

Is that where you find yourself? Are some of you saying, "This is my problem; it is always the self-life, the self-comfort, the self-consciousness, the self-pleasing, and the self-will; how can I get rid of it?" My answer is, It is Christ Jesus who can rid you of it; only Christ Jesus can give deliverance from the power of self. And what does He ask you to do? He asks that you should humble yourself before Him.

# 7

# *Absolute Surrender*

*"And Ben-hadad the king of Syria gathered all his host together . . . and he went up and besieged Samaria, and warred against it. And he sent messengers to Ahab king of Israel into the city, and said unto him, Thus saith Ben-hadad, thy silver and thy gold is mine; thy wives also and thy children, even the goodliest, are mine. And the king of Israel answered and said, My lord, O king, according to thy saying, I am thine, and all that I have"* (1 Kings 20:1–4).

What Ben-hadad asked for was *absolute surrender;* what Ahab gave was what was asked of him—*absolute surrender.* I want to use these words: "My lord, O king, according to thy saying, I am thine, and all that I have," as the words of absolute surrender which every believer should render to God. We have stated it before but it merits repeating—the absolute surrender of everything into His hands. Praise God! if our hearts are willing for that, there is no end to what God will do for us and to the blessing He will bestow.

*Absolute surrender*—let me tell you where I discovered this word. I have used it often and you may be familiar with it. Some time ago, in Scotland, I was discussing the condition of the Church with a group of Christian workers. In our group there was a godly worker whose main ministry was that of training workers. I asked him what he thought was the great

75

need of the Church and the message that should be preached. He answered very quietly and simply and determinedly: *"Absolute surrender to God is the one thing."* The words struck me as never before. He went on to tell that if the workers he trains are sound on that point, even though they may be backward, they are willing to be taught and always improve; whereas, those who are not totally surrendered very often go back and leave the work. The condition for obtaining God's full blessing is *absolute surrender* to Him.

I desire by God's grace to make this point unquestionably clear—God in heaven answers your prayers for spiritual blessing by this one demand: *Are you willing to surrender yourself absolutely into His hands?* What is our answer to be? God knows the hearts who have said it and those others who long to say it but hardly dare to do so. And there are hearts who have said it and yet have miserably failed, who feel condemned because they did not find the secret of the power to live that life. May God have a word for us all!

Let me say, first of all, *God claims it from us.* Yes, it has its foundation in the very nature of God. God cannot do otherwise. Who is God? He is the Fountain of life, the only Source of existence and power and goodness. Throughout the universe there is nothing good but what God works. God has created the sun, the moon, the stars, the flowers, the trees, and the grass; and are they not all absolutely surrendered to God? Do they not allow God to work in them just what He pleases? When God clothes the lily with its beauty, is it not yielded, surrendered, given over to God as He works in it its beauty? And God's redeemed children, oh, do you imagine that God can accomplish His work in you if there is only half or a part of your life surrendered? *God cannot do it.* God is life, and love, and blessing, and power, and infinite beauty, and God delights to communicate himself to every believer who is prepared to receive Him; but any lack of absolute surrender is just the thing that hinders God. Still He comes to you and as God He claims it.

You know in daily life what absolute surrender is. You

know that everything has to be surrendered to its special purpose and service. I have a pen in my pocket which is absolutely surrendered to its purpose of writing and must be absolutely surrendered to my hand if I am to write properly with it. If another holds it partly, I cannot write properly. My coat is absolutely yielded to me to cover my body. This building is entirely yielded to religious services. And now, do you expect that in your immortal being, in the divine nature that you have received by regeneration, God can accomplish His work, every day and every hour, unless you are entirely surrendered to Him? *God cannot.* The temple of Solomon was absolutely surrendered to God when it was dedicated to Him. And each of us is a temple of God, in which God will dwell and work mightily on one condition: absolute surrender to Him. God claims it, God is worthy of it, and without it God cannot accomplish His blessed work in us.

But secondly, God not only claims it, *but God will work it himself.* I am sure many believers say: Ah, but that absolute surrender implies so much! Recently I received a note from someone which read, "Oh, I have passed through so much trial and suffering, and there is so much of the self-life still remaining; I dare not face the entire surrender of it because I know it will cause so much trouble and agony." Alas! alas! that believers have such thoughts of Him, such cruel thoughts. Oh, I come to you with this message: God does not ask you to make a full surrender in your strength or by the power of your will; God is willing to work it in you. Do we not read, "It is God that worketh in us, both to will and to do of His good pleasure"? And that is our great need— to go on our faces before God until our hearts learn to believe that the everlasting God himself will come into our lives to change what is wrong, to conquer what is evil, and to work what is well-pleasing in His blessed sight. God himself will work it in you.

Look at the men in the Old Testament. Do you think it was by accident that God found a man like Abraham, the father of the faithful and the friend of God? Do you think it was Abraham himself, apart from God, who had such faith and obedience and devotion? You know it is not so. God raised him up and prepared him as an instrument for His glory. Did not God say to Pharaoh, "For this cause have I raised thee up, for to show in thee my power"? And if God said that of him, will not God say *it far more of every child of His?* Oh, I want to encourage you to cast away every fear. Come with that feeble desire; and if there is fear that your desire is not strong enough and that you cannot handle everything that may come, learn to know and trust your God. Say: "My God, I am willing that You should make me willing." If there is anything holding you back, or any sacrifice you are afraid of making, come to God and prove how gracious your God is. Never be afraid that He will command from you what He will not bestow! God comes and offers to work this absolute surrender in you. All these searchings and hungerings are longings that are in your heart. I tell you they are the drawings of the divine magnet, Christ Jesus. He who lived a life of absolute surrender is living in your heart by His Holy Spirit. You may have hindered Him terribly in the past, but He purposes through your humiliation and waiting upon Him to help you find full surrender. He comes and draws you by His message and words. Will you not come and trust God to work in you that absolute surrender to himself? Yes, blessed be God, He can and will do it.

The third thought. God not only claims it and works it, but *God accepts it when we bring it to Him.* God works it in the secret of our heart, urges us by the hidden power of His Holy Spirit to come and speak it out, and we must bring and yield to Him that absolute surrender. But remember, when you come and bring God that absolute surrender, it may, as far as your feelings or your consciousness go, be a thing of great imperfection. You may doubt and hesitantly say, "Is it absolute?" But remember the man to whom Christ said, "If thou canst believe, all things are possible to him that believeth"; his heart was afraid and he cried out, "Lord, I believe, help thou mine unbelief." That was a faith that triumphed over the devil and the demon was cast out. If you come and say, "Lord, I yield myself in absolute surrender to my God," even though it be with a trembling heart and with the consciousness, "I do not feel the power, I do not feel the determination, I do not feel the assurance," it will succeed. Do not be afraid to come just as you are, and even in the midst of your trembling, the power of the Holy Spirit will work.

Have you never learned the lesson that the Holy Spirit works with mighty power even when on the human side everything appears feeble? Look at the Lord Jesus Christ in Gethsemane. We read that He, "through the Eternal Spirit," offered himself as a sacrifice to God. The Almighty Spirit of God was enabling Him to do it. And yet what agony and fear and exceeding sorrow came over Him, and how He prayed! Externally you can see no sign of the mighty power of the Spirit, but the Spirit of God was there. Even so, while you are feeble and fighting and trembling, in faith in the hidden work of God's Spirit, do not fear, but yield yourself.

The first step in absolute surrender is to believe that God accepts it. That is the great point that we so often miss— believers should be occupied with God in this matter of sur- render. I pray you, *be occupied with God*. We want God to be clearer to us in our daily life, to have the right place, and be "all in all." To experience this we must look away from our- selves and look up to God. Though you may feel like a poor worm on earth and a trembling child of God full of failure and sin and fear, still bow and in simplicity say, "O God, I accept Your terms; I have pleaded for blessing on myself and others. I have accepted Your terms of absolute surrender." While your heart says that in deep silence, remember there is a God present that takes note of it and writes it down in His book; there is a God present who at that very moment takes possession of you. You may not feel it, you may not realize it, but God takes possession if you will trust Him. Oh, believers, who can estimate the work that can be done in and through the Church if we would individually and collectively say, I make an absolute surrender to my God.

A fourth thought. God not only claims it, works it, and accepts it when I bring it, but *God maintains it*. That is the great difficulty with many. People say: I have often been stirred at a meeting and I have consecrated myself to God, but it has passed away. It may last for a week or for a month, but it fades away and after a time is completely gone.

But listen! It does not have to be this way. When God has begun the work of absolute surrender in you, when He has accepted your surrender, then He promises to care for it and to keep it. Will you believe that?

In this matter of surrender both *God and I* are involved— I a worm, God the everlasting and omnipotent Jehovah. Worm, will you be afraid to trust yourself to this mighty God? God is willing. One of God's servants recently pleaded in prayer that each of us might hear His voice asking us, "Do you believe that I can do this, that I can keep you continually, day by day, and moment by moment?" What have you sung in that beautiful chorus?

> Moment by moment I'm *kept* in His love;
> Moment by moment I've life from above.

If God allows the sun to shine upon you moment by moment, without intermission, will not God let His life shine upon you every moment? And why have you not experienced it? Because you have not trusted God for it and you do not surrender yourself absolutely to God in that trust.

A life of absolute surrender has its difficulties. I do not deny that. Yes, it has something far more than difficulties; it is a life that with men is absolutely impossible. But by the grace of God, by the power of the Holy Spirit dwelling in us, it is a life to which we are destined and is possible for us, praise God! Let us believe that God will maintain it. Perhaps you have read the words of the aged George Müller who, on his ninetieth birthday, told of all God's goodness to him. What did he say was the secret of his happiness and of all the blessing with which God had given him? He said he believed there were two reasons. The one was that he had been enabled by grace to maintain a clear conscience before God day by day; the other was that he was a lover of God's Word. Ah, yes, a clear conscience in sincere obedience to God day by day, and fellowship with God every day in His Word and prayer—that is a life of absolute surrender.

Such a life has two sides—on the one side, *absolute surrender to work what God wants me to do;* on the other side, *to let God work what He wants to do.*

First, *to do what God wants me to do.* Surrender yourselves absolutely to the will of God. You may not know everything about God's will, but with what you do know say absolutely to the Lord God: "By Your grace I desire to do Your will in everything, every moment of every day." Say: "Lord God, not a word upon my tongue but for Your glory, not a movement of my temper but for Your glory, not an affection of love or hate in my heart but for Your glory and according to Your blessed will." Someone says, "Do you think that possible?" I ask, What has God promised? What can God do with a vessel absolutely surrendered to Him? Oh, God waits to bless us in a way beyond what we expect. "It is written, Eye hath not seen, nor ear heard, neither have entered into the heart of man, the things which God hath prepared for them that love Him." God has prepared unheard-of things, things you never can think of; blessings much more wonderful than you can imagine, more mighty than you can conceive. They are divine blessings. Come and say: "I give myself absolutely to God, to His will, to do only what God wants." It is God who will enable you to carry out the surrender.

And, on the other side, come and say: "I give myself absolutely to God, *to let Him work in me to will and to do of His good pleasure,* as He has promised to do." Yes, the living God wants to work in believers in a way that we cannot understand, but that God's Word nevertheless has revealed, and He wants to work in us every moment of the day. God is willing to maintain our life; only let our absolute surrender be one of simple, childlike, and unbounded trust.

The last thought. This absolute surrender to God *will wonderfully bless us.* What Ahab said to his enemy, King

Ben-hadad, "My lord, O king, according to thy word I am thine, and all that I have," shall we not say this to our God and loving Father? If we do say it, God's blessing will come upon us. God calls you to be separate from the world and the things that He hates. Come out and say: *"Lord, anything for You."* If you say that with prayer and speak it into God's ear, He will accept it and teach you what it means.

I say again, God will bless you. Have you been praying for blessing? Remember, there must be absolute surrender. Can God fill you, can God bless you, if you are not absolutely surrendered to Him? He cannot. Let us believe God has wonderful blessings for us, and say, be it with trembling will yet with a believing heart, "O God, I accept Your demands. I am Yours and all that I have. Absolute surrender is what my soul yields to You by divine grace."

Humble yourselves in God's sight and acknowledge that you have grieved the Holy Spirit by your self-will, self-confidence and self-effort. Bow humbly before Him in that confession and ask Him to break your heart and to bring you into the dust before Him. Then, as you bow before Him, receive God's teaching that in your flesh "there dwelleth no good thing" and that nothing will help you except another life which must come in. You must deny self once for all. Denying self must every moment be the power of your life and then Christ will come in and take possession of you.

When was Peter delivered? When was the change accomplished? The change began with Peter weeping; then the Holy Spirit came and filled his heart. God the Father loves to give us the power of the Spirit. We have the Spirit of God dwelling within us. We come to God confessing that and praising God for it; and yet confessing how we have grieved the Spirit. And then we bow our knees to the Father to ask that He would strengthen us with all might by the Spirit in the inner man, and that He would fill us with His mighty power. As the Spirit reveals Christ to us, Christ comes to live in our hearts forever, and the self-life is cast out.

As we bow before God in humiliation, in that humiliation we want to also confess before Him the condition of the whole

Church. No words can fully express this sadness. I wish I had words to speak what I sometimes feel about it. Just think of the believers around you. I am not speaking of nominal believers or of those professing faith, but I speak of those honest, sincere believers who are not living a life in the power of God or to His glory. So little power, so little devotion or consecration to God, so little conception of the truth that a believer is a man utterly surrendered to God's will! Oh, we want to confess the sins of God's people around us and to humble ourselves. We are members of a sick body, and the sickliness of the body will hinder and break us down unless we come to God and in confession separate ourselves from partnership with worldliness, with coldness toward each other, unless we surrender ourselves wholly for God.

How much is being done in the spirit of the flesh and in the power of self! How much work, day by day, in which human energy—our will and our thoughts about the work— is continually manifested and in which there is very little waiting upon God for the power of the Holy Spirit! Let us make confession. But as we confess the feebleness and sinfulness of work for God among us, let us come back to ourselves. Do you truly desire to be delivered from the power of the self-life? Have you acknowledged the power of self and the flesh and been willing to cast it all at the feet of Christ? *There is deliverance.*

Remember: Death was the path to glory for Christ. For the joy set before Him He endured the cross. The cross was the birthplace of His everlasting glory. Do you love Christ? Do you long to be *in* Christ and not *like* Him? Let death be to you the most desirable thing on earth; death to self and fellowship with Christ. Separation—do you think it a hard thing to be entirely free from the world and by that separation be united to God and His love, by separation to become prepared for living and walking with God every day? Surely we should say, "Anything to bring me to separation, to death, for a life of full fellowship with God and Christ." Oh! come and cast this self-life and flesh-life at the feet of Jesus. Then trust Him. Do not try to understand it all, but come in the living faith that Christ will come into you with the power of His death and the power of His life; then the Holy Spirit will bring the whole Christ—Christ crucified and Christ risen and living in glory—into your heart.

# 8

## *Christ Our Life*

*"Christ, who is our life"* (Col. 3:4).

I know that many who have made an absolute surrender have felt as I have felt: O God, how little we understand it! and that they have prayed, "Lord God, You must truly take possession if we are to know what it really means." It has been stated that we believe that through our faith God does accept our surrender, although the experience and the power of that absolute surrender may not come at once, and that we are to hold fast our faith in God until the experience and power do come.

But let me now add what has only been mentioned before: *if this absolute surrender is to be maintained and lived out, it must be by having Christ coming into our life in new power.* That is the thought I wish to address now. It is only in Christ that we can draw near to God, and it is only in Christ that God can draw near to us. We need to have "Christ our life." We often plead with God to work mightily in the Church and in the world, in the power of the Holy Spirit for the sanctification of His people and for the conversion of sinners. What we need is that *what we ask God to do in others would be fully done in ourselves.* We need to allow Christ to take entire possession of us, and then Christ will be able to work through us above what we ask or think.

To illustrate this great truth of "Christ our life," I want to use four very simple thoughts. If we want to understand those words, let us consider, first, *Christ before us as our example;* secondly, *Christ for us as our propitiation;* thirdly, *Christ with us as our Savior from sin;* and lastly, *Christ in us as our strength and our life.* "O Lord, give Your grace that these human words may not cover us with any covering but the covering of Your Spirit. Lord God, awaken in our hearts the realization that we are all children of Your family, bowing before Your feet. Awaken in every heart a deep faith that our God, by the Holy Spirit, is going to reveal Christ to us even now. Our Father, we wait on You. Our soul waits and our hope is in Your Word."

If Christ is to be our life, we must initially look at *Christ before us as our example.* When I speak of Christ as my life, it must not be a vague generalization, but I must *know.* Life always works itself out in conduct and action; if Christ comes into me as my life, it must not only be something hidden in my heart, but something that proves itself in every action and in every moment of my existence. If I want to know how it will show itself, what my attitudes and words and actions and habits will be if I have Christ's life, I must go to the life of the Lord Jesus upon earth and study that. As I study the life and walk of God's beloved Son, I must remember that one of the reasons that God sent Jesus to live upon earth was that in His life I might have a picture, a revelation, a complete representation of what God wanted me to be and was willing to make me. That is the light in which we should study the life of Christ in the Gospels—not the only light, but perhaps the most important light.

What do I find, then, as I look at Christ? I find absolute surrender to God. That was the very root of Christ's life. He came as a man whom God had sent into the world, and as a man whose only purpose was to fulfill the will of God. He came as a man who had nothing in himself, but who every day depended upon God and waited for God to teach Him, to speak words through Him, and to show Him the works He had to do. "The Son can do nothing of himself." He lived a life of absolute surrender to God. God's will, God's honor, God's kingdom—He lived and He died for them. He did not do it under strain at certain times, throwing it off at other times to seek relaxation in something of the world and forgetting to hold communion with God, as many believers do. Religion is often seen as a strain, a burden, a duty, and it is so delightful just to relax a little and throw off the strain. Ah, no! God was Christ's joy and the fountain of living waters to Him; it was His delight and His strength to live in God and for God. The will of God was His meat and refreshment and strength.

And God comes to all of us who are asking: "My God, I have made an absolute surrender, and You know that though it was done in feebleness and trembling, it was done in honesty and in uprightness; but, my God, what does it mean? How am I to live that life?" The Father points to the beloved Son and says, "This is my beloved Son, in whom I am well pleased. Hear Him, follow Him, live like Him, let Christ be the law of your life."

Let us yield our hearts to God in prayer, for Him to search and discover to us whether the life of Christ has actually been the law that we have taken for the guide of our life. I am not speaking about attainment, but let us ask, Have I actually said, "Oh, how blessed it would be! Oh, this is what I desire and wait upon God for! It almost sounds as if it is too high and presumptous"? But what did Christ mean when He said so often, "As I, even so you; as I loved, even so love one another; as I kept the commandments of my Father, so, if ye keep His commandments, ye shall abide in my love"? What does the Holy Spirit mean when He says, "Let this mind be in you, which was also in Christ Jesus . . . who made himself of no reputation . . . but humbled himself, and became obedient unto death"? The mind of Christ must be my mind, my disposition, and my life.

Many people want eternal life in heaven but do not want the life here on earth which Christ lived. There are many believers who have stated, "There can be no thought of im-

itating and following Christ with any degree of exactness."
Their goal is not to come near to Christ. But if you honestly
have given your heart in absolute surrender to God, then
come and say, "The life of Christ must become mine."

Second, if we want to know what this means, "Christ our
life," we must not only look at Christ and His work before
us as our example, but *Christ for us as our propitiation*. In
His life Christ prepared the path in which we are to walk.
He left us an example that we should follow in His footsteps;
He marked out the road we were to travel on the way to
eternal life. But that was not enough, for we were shut out
from the path and that life by sin and its curse, death. And
so Christ, after having prepared and marked out the blessed
path, went down into the suffering and the death of Calvary,
yielding His will to God unto the death. There He bore our
sins and our curse, the chastisement of our peace was laid
upon Him, that by His stripes we might be healed. He gave
His precious blood, "the blood of the everlasting covenant,"
that by it He might gain an entrance for us into the very
presence of our God. Now Christ is there as our High Priest,
to apply within our hearts, as a living Savior, the divine
power of that propitiation. Whenever we think of drawing
near to God, of serving God and of offering ourselves to God,
the thought comes up: In my sinfulness, with my transgressions and backslidings since I was converted and received
Christ, can I actually have fellowship with God every day?
The answer comes: We have been "made nigh by the blood
of Jesus." "Having . . . boldness by the blood of Jesus, let us
draw near."

Have any of you felt afraid to make the absolute surrender because you felt too unworthy? Consider this: Your worthiness is not in yourself or in the intensity or uprightness
of your consecration; *your worthiness is in Christ Jesus*. We
read in God's Word, it is "the altar that sanctifieth the gift,"
and we know that Christ is not only the Priest and "the Lamb
that was slain," but that the living Christ himself is the
altar. Seven days the altar was to be sanctified by a sevenfold

blood sprinkling; after that God said, "That altar shall be an altar most holy: whatsoever toucheth the altar shall be holy." And in the New Testament we are taught that "the altar sanctifieth the gift." Christ is our altar. Oh, if there is anyone afraid and asking, "Can God accept me in my feebleness?" come and be not afraid. Lay yourself upon Christ, the living altar, the everlasting propitiation, who alone can make you acceptable to God every moment, and rest there. Rest upon Him in sweet consciousness and faith. All unworthy and all feeble though I be, the altar sanctifies the gift; in Jesus, resting on Him, my God accepts my feebleness and I am well pleasing in His sight. Oh, believers, seek to maintain this truth, not only as a doctrine for the comfort and salvation of the unconverted, declaring full and immediate pardon, but seek to maintain it as the power of continual access to God. "If we walk in the light . . . the blood of Jesus Christ his Son cleanseth us from all sin." It is in Christ that the door to the heart of my Father is open every moment; it is in the blood of the blessed Lamb of God that every moment the inflowing of the divine life can come into your heart and mine.

Third, I not only have Christ before me as my example, and Christ for me as my propitiation, but I have *Christ with me as my Savior from sin, my friend, my leader, and my guide.* Yes, that was the precious promise of our gracious Lord before He left. "Lo, I am with you alway." Earlier than that He had said, when the disciples did not yet understand Him, "Where two or three are gathered together in my name, there I am in the midst of them."

What you and I need to realize is this: Jesus Christ is nearer to us than our nearest earthly friend. Ah! if we only took the time to turn our eyes and hearts away from this world, even from the loving faces and friends that surround us, and all the joys that attract us and all the love that greets us; if we were to fix them steadfastly and humbly and trustingly on the face and the love and the joy of Jesus, He would be able to so manifest himself to our hearts that we would be filled with the consciousness that *Jesus is with me.* You know how deep in the consciousness of a father, every morning as he rises, is the thought: I have beloved children, I have a beloved wife, I have a family; we meet at breakfast. It is so natural; the whole heart is so full of it that it does not need a conscious thought. Can it be that Christ can make His presence as near and as clear and as dear to me as the fellowship of the dearest ones upon earth? *Christ can do it and longs to do it and is worthy that we should let Him do it.* O God, when will the time come when Your Son will be nearer to us than father or mother, wife or husband, child or brother? Oh, hasten that blessed hour!

Jesus Christ wants to live and to walk with you that He may do this blessed work for you. He wants to be with you as your companion, so that you never shall be alone. There is no trial, no difficulty, no fire, no water through which you have to pass, but in which the promise of Jehovah in the Old Testament, "I will be with thee," will not be fulfilled to you in Christ Jesus. No battle that you have to fight with sin or temptation, no feebleness that makes you tremble in the consciousness of what you are yourself, but it is possible to have Christ at your side every moment—Jesus Christ as leader, to show you the way you should walk; Jesus Christ as companion, to comfort you by His presence and make your heart glad; Jesus Christ as Savior from sin, in His mighty power watching over you and working in you all God's good pleasure. Oh, that God might show us that the life of absolute surrender is a life that can be lived in Christ Jesus, a life that can be lived because Christ himself will care for us and watch over us.

Then comes the last thought: *Christ in us as our life and our strength.* That is the crown of all. New believers usually understand very little of this. Many believers have had some experience of Christ with them as guide and helper, but have not come to realize what this other means: Christ in me, my very life and strength. And yet that is what the Apostle Paul tells us is the great gospel mystery, the mystery that was hid for generations, but has now been revealed; the mystery of God's people, of which he says "the riches of the glory of this mystery, which is Christ in you." Believers, the riches and glory of our God are manifest to you in this: God wants you to have Christ His Son living in you. May we come, then, not asking for a little blessing, a beginning of blessings, but to have our whole life opened up to the indwelling, controlling, sanctifying power of Jesus Christ.

I would like to address Christian workers. Our great thought has been that of *work*. But what is needed if God is to bless His workers? How is God's power to come and to work? Beloved, Christ is the power of God and we need more of Christ, we need the whole Christ, we need Christ revealed in us by the Holy Spirit; then the power of God will work.

We referred to a church so filled with the Holy Spirit that He could say to that church: "Set apart for me the men that I have called for my work." We spoke of workers as people who are ready and willing to be set apart for the Holy Spirit. How can each church be brought to this condition? In one way only. John the Baptist preached Christ who baptized "with the Holy Ghost and with fire." That tells me Jesus Christ is the one from whom the Holy Spirit must come in ever new and larger measure; if you want the power of God's Spirit to be revealed in and through the Church, it must come from a closer attachment to Christ, a closer union with Him, a larger revelation of Christ dwelling in believers. A blessing then must come. Did not Jesus say, "He that believeth on me, out of him shall flow rivers of living water"? And is not this by faith, *by believing that Christ comes and dwells in the heart,* and becomes the fountain out of which the Holy Spirit flows? What do we read in the last chapter of the Revelation of John? "And He showed me a pure river of water of life, clear as crystal, proceeding out of the throne of God and of the Lamb." Yes, when the Lamb sat down upon the throne of glory, the river of water of life flowed out. It is the Lamb who must lead us to the fountains of living water and give them within our hearts, so that we shall have power to work among men—not the power of reason, not the power of human love, zeal, earnestness, and diligence, but the power that comes from God.

Are you ready for that power? Are you ready to surrender yourself absolutely to God and receive it? Can you truly say: "Lord, I am totally surrendered to You. It is done feebly, tremblingly, but, Lord God, it is done. I have received a small portion of what I know You can give, but as an empty vessel, cleansed and humble, I place myself at Your feet again, day by day and moment by moment, and I wait upon You"? And, believer, what no eye has seen nor ear heard, what men have never been able to conceive, what you have not conceived, God will do for them that wait for Him, for them that love Him.

Church life will profit us very little unless it leads us closer to God, to have larger expectations from God, and closer fellowship with God. How can that be? Christ Jesus can do it for us. Christ is our life. He will live in us the same life He lived upon earth. Shall we not expect Him to do it in the fullness of His promise? Shall we not come with every sin, every hindrance, every shortcoming, everything that causes self-condemnation, and cast it all at His feet, believing that the blood cleanses and Jesus gives deliverance? Believe, expect and accept that God will reveal Christ within us in the power of the Holy Spirit. God grant it to every believer.

# 9

## *We Can Love All the Day*

*"The fruit of the Spirit is love"* (Gal. 5:22).

You can easily understand why I chose this subject. We have addressed the great need for believers to be brought together and united in one spirit and one body. We said that one of the great reasons why God cannot bless is *the lack of love* in the Church. When the body is divided, there cannot be strength.

Going to Holland brings this thought to mind. In the time of their great religious wars, when the country stood out so nobly against Spain, one of their mottos was: "Unity gives strength." The same is true for us. Only when believers stand as one body, one before God in the fellowship of love, one toward another in deep affection, one before the world in a love that the world can see—only then will they have power to secure the blessing which they ask from God. Remember, a vessel that is cracked into many pieces cannot be filled. You can take a piece of a broken vessel and dip out a little water with it, but if you want the vessel full, the vessel must be whole. That is literally true of Christ's Church, and if there is one thing we still must pray for it is this: "Lord melt us together into one by the power of the Holy Spirit; let the Holy Spirit, who at Pentecost made them all one heart and one soul, do His blessed work among us." Praise God, we can love each other in a divine love, for "the fruit of the Spirit is love." Yield yourselves to love and the Holy Spirit will come; receive the Spirit and He will teach you to love more.

Now, why is it that the fruit of the Spirit is love? *Because God is love.* And what does that mean? It is the very nature and being of God to delight in communicating himself. God has no selfishness, God keeps nothing to himself. *God's nature is to be always giving.* In the sun, the moon, and the stars, in every flower you see it, in every bird in the air, in every fish in the sea. God communicates life to His creatures. And the angels around His throne, the seraphim and cherubim who are flames of fire—where does their glory come from? It is because God is love and imparts some of His brightness and His blessedness to them. And we, His redeemed children—God delights to pour out His love into us. Why? Because, as I said, God keeps nothing for himself. From eternity God had His only begotten Son. The Father gave Him all things, and nothing that God had was kept back. "God is love."

One of the old Church Fathers said that the best way to understand the Trinity was through the revelation of divine love—the Father, the loving one, the fountain of love; the Son, the beloved one, the reservoir of love in whom the love was poured out; and the Spirit, the living love that united both and then overflowed into this world. The Spirit of Pentecost, the Spirit of the Father and the Spirit of the Son, is love. When the Holy Spirit comes to us and to other men, will He be less a Spirit of love than He is in God? It cannot be; He cannot change His nature. The Spirit of God is love, and "the fruit of the Spirit is love."

Why is that so? That was the one great need of mankind, that was the thing which Christ's redemption came to accomplish: *to restore love to this world.* When man sinned, why was it that he sinned? Selfishness triumphed—he sought self instead of God. And just look! Adam at once begins to accuse the woman of having led him astray. Love to God had gone, love to man was lost. Look again; of the first two children of

Adam, the one becomes a murderer of his brother. Does that not teach us that sin had robbed the world of love? Ah! what a proof the history of the world has been of love having been lost! The Lord Jesus Christ came from heaven as the Son of God's love. "God so loved the world that he gave his only begotten Son." God's Son demonstrated what love is, He lived a life of love here upon earth in fellowship with His disciples, in compassion over the poor and miserable, in love even to His enemies, and He died the death of love. And when He went to heaven, whom did He send down? The Spirit of love, to come and banish selfishness and envy and pride, and bring the love of God into the hearts of men. "The fruit of the Spirit is love."

And what was the preparation for the promise of the Holy Spirit? You remember that promise as found in John 16. But also remember what precedes in the thirteenth chapter. Before Christ promised the Holy Spirit, He gave a new commandment and said wonderful things about it. One thing was, "Even as I have loved you, so love ye one another." To them His dying love was to be the only law of their conduct and interaction with each other. What a message to those fishermen, to those men full of pride and selfishness! "Learn to love each other," said Christ, "as I have loved you." And by the grace of God they did it. When Pentecost came they were of one heart and one soul. Christ did it for them.

What more did He say? "By this shall all men know that ye are my disciples, if ye have love one to another." You all know what it is to wear a badge. Christ said to His disciples, in effect: "I give you a badge, and that badge is *love;* that is to be your mark. It is *the only thing* in heaven or on earth by which men can know me." Should we not fear that *love has fled from the earth*? If we were to ask the world if it has seen us wear the badge of *love,* what would its answer be? As the world views the Church of Christ, can it find a place where there is no quarrelling and separation? Let us ask God with one heart that we may wear the badge of Jesus, *love.* God is able to give it.

"The fruit of the Spirit is love." Why? *Because nothing*

*but love can expel and conquer our selfishness.* Self is the great curse, whether in its relation to God or toward others—thinking of ourselves and seeking our own. Self is our greatest curse. But, praise God, Christ came to redeem us from self. We sometimes talk about deliverance from the self-life, and we should praise God for every word that can be said to help us. But I am afraid some people think deliverance from the self-life means this: Now I am going to have no more troubles within myself in serving God. And they forget that *deliverance from the self-life means to be a vessel overflowing with love to everybody all the day.*

Here we have the reason why so many people pray for the power of the Holy Spirit and yet receive so little. They prayed for power for work and for blessing, but they have not prayed for power for full deliverance from self. That means not only the righteous self in relationship with God, but the unloving self in relationship with men. But there is deliverance. "The fruit of the Spirit is love." I bring you the glorious promise that Christ is able to fill our hearts with love.

Many of us try hard at times to love. We try to force ourselves to love and I am not saying that is wrong; it is better than nothing. But the result is always very sad. Continual failure is its fruit. Why? The reason is simply this: I have never learned to believe and accept the truth that the Holy Spirit can pour out God's love into my heart. How often we have limited this blessed text: "The love of God is shed abroad in our hearts." It is often understood in the sense that it means the love of God *to me.* Oh, what a limitation! That is only the beginning. The love of God always means the love of God in its entirety, in its fullness as an indwelling power, a love of God to me that leaps back to Him in love, and overflows to others in love—God's love to me, my love to God, and my love to others. The three are one; you cannot separate them. Do believe that the love of God can be so shed abroad in our hearts that we can love all the day.

"Ah," you say, "how little I have understood that!" Why is a lamb always gentle? Because that is its nature. Does it cost the lamb any trouble to be gentle? No. Why not? It *is* so beautiful and gentle. Does a lamb study to be gentle? No. Why does that come so easy? It is its nature. And a wolf— why does it cost a wolf no trouble to be cruel, to put its fangs into the poor lamb or sheep? Because that is its nature. It does not have to summon up its courage; the wolf-nature is there.

So how can I learn to love? I cannot until the Spirit of God fills my heart with God's love and I begin to long for God's love in a very different sense from which I have sought it so selfishly: as a comfort and a joy and a happiness and a pleasure to myself. I cannot until I begin to learn that "God is love," and claim and receive it as an indwelling power for self-sacrifice. I cannot until I begin to see that my glory, my blessedness, is to be like God and like Christ in yielding everything in myself for others. May God teach us that! Oh, the divine blessedness of the love with which the Holy Spirit can fill our hearts! "The fruit of the Spirit is love."

Once again I ask, Why must this be so? And my answer is: *Without this we cannot live the daily life of love.* When we speak about the consecrated life, we often speak about *temper*, and some have said, "You make too much of temper." I do not think we can make too much of it. When we look at a clock, we know what the hands mean. The hands tell us what is within the clock, and if I see that the hands are not moving or that the clock is slow or fast, I say there is something inside the clock that is wrong. Temper is just like the revelation that the clock gives of what is within. Temper is a proof of whether the love of Christ is filling the heart. Many find it easier in church or prayer meeting, or witnessing for the Lord, to be holy and happy than in the daily life with their wife and children; easier to be holy and happy outside of the home than in it. Where is the love of God? In Christ. God has prepared a wonderful redemption in Christ and longs to make something supernatural of us. Have we learned to desire it, to ask for it, and to expect it in its fullness?

Then there is the *tongue*! Just think what liberty many believers give to their tongues. They say, "I have a right to think and say what I like." When they speak about each other, when they speak about their neighbors, when they speak about other believers, how often these are sharp remarks! God keep me from saying anything that would be unloving; God shut my mouth if I am not speaking in tender love. But what I am saying is a fact. How often we find believers who though banded together in work are still full of sharp criticism, sharp judgment, hasty opinion, unloving words, secret contempt of each other, secret condemnation of each other. Oh, do we believe that just as a mother's love covers her children, delights in them, and has the tenderest compassion upon them despite their failures, so there should be in the heart of every believer a motherly love toward every brother and sister in Christ? Have you aimed at that? Have you sought it? Have you ever pleaded for it? Jesus Christ said, "As I have loved you . . . love one another." He did not put that among the other commandments, but He said in effect, "That is a new commandment, the one commandment: love one another as I have loved you."

What is the reason that the Holy Spirit cannot come in power? Is it possible? You remember the comparison I used in speaking of the vessel. I can dip a little water into a broken piece of the vessel, but if a vessel is to be full it must be unbroken. Wherever believers come together, to whatever church or mission or society they belong, they must love each other intensely or the Spirit of God cannot do His work. We talk about grieving the Spirit of God by worldliness, ritualism, formality, error and indifference, but, I tell you, the greatest thing that grieves God's Spirit is this lack of love. Let us ask God to search our hearts regarding a love like His.

Why are we taught that "the fruit of the Spirit is love"? *Because the Spirit of God has come to make our daily life a demonstration of divine power and a revelation of what God can do for His children.* Think of the Church at large. What divisions! Think of the different bodies. Take the question of holiness, of the cleansing blood, of the baptism of the Spirit—

what differences are caused among dear believers by such questions! That there should be differences of opinion does not trouble me. But how often hate, bitterness, contempt, separation, and unlovingness have surrounded the holiest truths of God's Word! It was so in the time of the Reformation between the Lutheran and Calvinistic churches. What bitterness there was then in regard to the Lord's Supper, which was meant to be the bond of union between all believers! And so, down through the ages, the very dearest truths of God have become mountains that have separated us. If we want to pray in power, if we desire the Holy Spirit to come down in power and to be poured out, we must covenant with God that we will love one another with a heavenly love. Are you ready for that? Only true love is large enough to take in all God's children, even the most unloving, unlovable, unworthy, unbearable and trying. If our absolute surrender to God was true, then it must mean absolute surrender to the divine love to fill me; to be a servant of love to love every child of God around me. "The fruit of the Spirit is love."

God did something wonderful when He gave the glorified Christ the Holy Spirit to come down out of the heart of the Father and His everlasting love. And how we have degraded the Holy Spirit into a mere power by which we carry on our work! God forgive us. Oh, that the Holy Spirit might be held in honor as a power to fill us with the very life and nature of God and of Christ! "The fruit of the Spirit is love."

I ask once again, Why is it so? And the answer comes: *That is the only power in which Christians really can do their work.* Yes, this is what we need. We need love to bind us to each other as well as a divine love in our work for the lost around us. Do we not often undertake a great deal of work just as men undertake the work of philanthropy, from a natural spirit of compassion for others? Do we not often undertake Christian work because our minister or friend calls us to it, and do we not often perform Christian work with a certain zeal without having had a baptism of love?

People often ask, What is the baptism of fire? I have answered that I know no fire like the fire of God, the fire of everlasting love that consumed the sacrifice on Calvary. The baptism of love is what the Church needs; to receive it we must begin at once to get down upon our faces before God in confession and plead: "Lord, let love from heaven flow down into my heart. I am yielding my life to pray and live as one who has surrendered himself for the everlasting love to dwell in and fill." Ah yes, if the love of God were in our hearts, what a difference it would make! There are many who say, "I work for Christ, and I feel I could work much more but I have not the gift; I do not know how or where to begin, I do not know what I can do." Brother, sister, ask God to baptize you with the Spirit of love, and love will find its way. Love is a fire that will burn through every difficulty. You may be a shy, hesitating person who cannot speak well, but love can burn through everything. God fill us with love! We need it for our work.

You may have read touching stories of this love expressed. I heard one not long ago. Mrs. Butler had been asked to speak at a Rescue Home where there were a number of poor women. Arriving there, she saw outside a wretched object sitting, and asked, "Who is that?" The matron answered, "She has been into the house thirty or forty times and has always gone away again; nothing can be done with her, she is so low and hard." But Mrs. Butler said, "She must come in." The matron then told Mrs. Butler: "We have been waiting for you, the people are assembled, and you only have an hour for the message." Mrs. Butler replied, "No, this is of more importance." She went outside where the woman was sitting and said, "My sister, what is the matter?" "I am not your sister," was the reply. Then Mrs. Butler laid her hand on her and said, "Yes, I am your sister, and I love you"; and so she spoke until the heart of the poor woman was touched. The conversation lasted some time and the people inside were waiting patiently. Finally Mrs. Butler brought the woman into the room. There was the poor wrecked, degraded creature, full of shame. She would not sit on a chair, but sat down on a stool beside Mrs. Butler's seat, and Mrs. Butler let her lean against her, with her arms around the poor woman's neck, while she spoke to the assembled people. It was that love which touched the woman's heart; she had found someone who really loved her, and that love gave access to the love of Jesus. Praise God! there is love upon earth in the hearts of God's children; but oh, that there were more!

I ask again, Why is it written that "the fruit of the Spirit is love"? *Because without love we cannot do our work.* May God baptize our ministers, our missionaries, our evangelists, our Sunday school teachers, and our young people's groups with a tender love. Oh, that God would begin with us now and baptize us with heavenly love!

Once again, *it is only love that can enable us for the work of intercession.* I have said that love must enable us for our work. Do you know what the hardest and the most important work is? It is the work of intercession, the work of going to God and taking time to lay hold on Him. A man may be an earnest believer, an earnest minister, and a man may do good, but alas! how often he must confess that he knows very little of what it is to wait upon God! May God give us that great gift of an intercessory spirit, a spirit of prayer and supplication! Let me ask you in the name of Jesus not to let a day pass without praying for all God's people.

I find there are believers who think little of that. I find prayer meetings where they pray for their own members, but not for all believers. Take time to pray for the Church of Christ. It is right to pray for the lost as I have already said. God help us to pray more for them. It is right to pray for missionaries and for evangelistic work. But Paul did not tell people to pray for the heathen or the unconverted. Paul told them to pray for believers. Make this your first prayer every day: *"Lord, bless Your saints everywhere."* The condition of Christ's Church is indescribably low. Plead for God's people that He would visit them, plead for each other, plead for all believers who are trying to work for God. Let love fill your heart. Ask Christ to pour love into you every day. Receive the Holy Spirit's instruction: *I am set apart to the Holy Spirit, and the fruit of the Spirit is love.* God help us to understand it.

We have often mentioned the place of waiting upon God. May God grant that we learn day by day to wait more quietly upon Him. If you wait upon God only for yourself, the power to do so will soon be lost; but give yourself to the ministry and the love of intercession, and pray more for God's people, for God's people round about you, for the Spirit of love in yourself and in them, and for the work of God you are connected with. The answer will surely come and your waiting upon God will be the source of untold blessing and power. "The fruit of the Spirit is love."

How shall I conclude? I think we must go to God again in intercession. Let us plead in faith that God may pour out a spirit of love upon us. Have you a lack of love to confess before God? Then make confession and say before Him: "O Lord, my lack of heart, my lack of love—I confess it." And then, as you cast that lack at His feet, believe that the blood cleanses you, that Jesus comes in His mighty cleansing, saving power to deliver you, and that He will give His Holy Spirit.

"THE FRUIT OF THE SPIRIT IS LOVE."

# 10

## *Impossible with Men, Possible with God*

*"And he said, The things which are impossible with men are possible with God"* (Luke 18:27).

Christ had said to the rich young ruler, "Sell all that thou hast . . . and come, follow me." The young man went away sorrowful. Christ turned to the disciples and said, "How hardly shall they that have riches enter into the kingdom of God!" The disciples, we read, were greatly astonished and answered, "If it is so difficult to enter the kingdom, who then can be saved?" And Christ gave this blessed answer: "The things which are impossible with men are possible with God."

By now we have prayed and listened to God's Word with humiliation and encouragement. What can we say to encourage each other to follow through on what God has spoken. I trust that this word will be full of faith and confidence, that the Holy Spirit will breathe it into our hearts, and that we shall go on with one thought: "The things which are impossible with men are possible with God." May God help us to open our ears and hearts to the blessed Lord Jesus until He speaks into the very depths of our being: "The things which are impossible with men are possible with God."

The text contains just two thoughts: (1) *Concerning sal-*

*vation and following Christ by a holy life, it is impossible for men to do it.* (2) *What is impossible with men is possible with God.* Let us look at these two sides.

The two thoughts mark the two great lessons that man has to learn in the spiritual life. It often takes a long time to learn the first lesson, that spiritually man can do nothing, that salvation is impossible to man. And often a man learns that, but yet he does not learn the second lesson—what has been impossible to me is possible with God. Blessed is the man who learns both lessons.

Learning these two lessons marks two stages in the Christian's life. The initial stage sees a man trying to do his utmost and failing, then trying to do still better and failing again, then trying still more and always failing. Unfortunately, he very often still does not learn the lesson: *It is impossible.* Peter spent three years in Christ's school and never learned that word, *It is impossible,* until he denied his Lord and went out and wept bitterly. Then he learned the lesson: *With man it is impossible to serve God and Christ.*

Just look for a moment at a man who is learning this lesson: *It is impossible with man.* At first he fights against it; then he submits to it, but reluctantly and in despair; at last he accepts it willingly and rejoices in it. At the beginning of the Christian life the new believer has no understanding of this truth. He has been converted, he has the joy of the Lord in his heart, he begins to run the race and fight the battle; he is sure he can conquer because he is sincere and honest and God will help him. Yet, somehow, very soon he fails where he did not expect it and sin gets the better of him. He is disappointed; but he thinks: I was not watchful enough, I did not make my commitments strong enough. So again he vows, again he prays, and yet he fails. He thinks: Am I not a regenerate man? Have I not the life of God within me? And he thinks again: Yes, and I have Christ to help me. I can live the holy life.

At a later period he comes to another stage. He sees that such a life is impossible, but he does not accept it. There are multitudes of believers who come to this point: I cannot do it, therefore God never expected me to do what I cannot do. If you tell them that God does expect it, it appears to them a mystery. Many live a life of failure and of sin instead of rest and victory because they begin to see: I cannot, it is impossible. And yet they do not understand it fully, and so, under the impression, *I cannot,* they give way to a thought of despair. They will do their best, but they never expect to be successful.

But God leads His children on to a third stage. This is when a man receives that word, *It is impossible,* in its full truth, and yet at the same time says, *I must do it and I will do it—it is impossible for man, and yet I must do it*; when the renewed will begins to exercise its whole power, and in intense longing and prayer begins to cry to God: "Lord, what does this mean?—how am I to be freed from the power of sin?" It is the state of the regenerate man in Romans 7. There you find the believer trying his very utmost to live a holy life. God's law has been revealed to him as reaching down into the very depth of the desires of the heart, and the man dares to say, "I delight in the law of God after the inward man. To will what is good is present with me. My heart loves the law of God and my will has chosen that law." Can a man like that fail, with his heart full of delight in God's law and with his will determined to do what is right? Yes. That is what Romans 7 teaches. There is something lacking. Not only must I delight in the law of God after the inward man and will what God wills, but I need a divine omnipotence to work it in me. That is what the Apostle Paul teaches in Philippians 2: "It is God which worketh in you, both to will and to do."

Note the contrast. In Romans 7 the regenerate man says, "To will is present with me, but to do—I find I cannot do. I will, but I cannot perform." But in Philippians 2 you have a man who has been led further, a man who understands that when God has worked the renewed will, He will give the power to accomplish what that will desires. Let us receive this as the first great lesson in the spiritual life: It is impossible for me; let there be an end of the flesh and all its powers, an end of self, and let it be my glory to be helpless. Praise God for the divine teaching that makes us helpless!

In *absolute surrender to God* we are meant to be brought to an end of ourselves and yet we may feel: I cannot see how I actually can live as absolutely surrendered to God every moment of the day—in my house, in my business, in the midst of trials and temptations. Here we need to learn the lesson: If you feel you cannot do it, you are on the right road. Accept that position and maintain it before God: "My heart's desire and delight, O God, is absolute surrender, but I cannot perform it. It is impossible for me to live that life; it is beyond me." Fall down and learn that when you are utterly helpless, God will come to work in you not only to will but also to do.

Now comes the second lesson: "The things which are impossible with men *are possible with God.*" Many learn the lesson, *It is impossible with men,* and then give up in helpless despair and live a wretched Christian life without joy, or strength, or victory. Why? Because they do not humble themselves to learn that other lesson: *With God all things are possible.*

Your daily spiritual life is to be a proof that God works impossibilities; your spiritual life is to be a series of impossibilities made possible and actual by God's almighty power. That is what the Christian needs. He has an almighty God whom he worships, and he must understand: I do not want a little of God's power, but I want—with reverence be it said—the whole of God's omnipotence to keep me and to live like Christ.

The whole of Christianity is a work of God's omnipotence. Look at the birth of Christ Jesus. That was a miracle of divine power as it was announced to Mary, "With God nothing shall be impossible." It was the omnipotence of God. Look at Christ's resurrection. We are taught that it was according to *the exceeding greatness of His almighty power* that God raised Christ from the dead.

Every tree must grow on the root from which it springs.

An oak tree three hundred years old grows on the same root from which it had its beginning. Christianity had its beginning in the omnipotence of God, and in every soul it must have its continuance in that omnipotence. All the possibilities for spiritual growth have their origin in a new apprehension of Christ's power to work all God's will in us. I want to call you to come and worship an almighty God. Have you learned to do it? Have you learned to deal so closely with the almighty God that you know omnipotence is working in you? Outwardly there may often be little sign of it. The Apostle Paul said, "I was with you in weakness and in fear and in much trembling, and . . . my preaching was . . . in demonstration of the Spirit and of power." From the human side there was feebleness; from the divine side there was divine omnipotence. And that is true of every godly life. If we would only learn that lesson better and give a wholehearted, undivided surrender to it, we would learn the blessing of dwelling every hour and every moment with the almighty God.

Have you ever studied the attribute of God's omnipotence? You know that it was God's omnipotence that created the world, light out of darkness, and man. But have you studied God's omnipotence in the works of redemption?

Look at Abraham. When God called him to be the father of that people from which Christ was to be born, God said to him, "I am the Almighty God; walk before me and be thou perfect." God trained Abraham to trust Him as the Omnipotent One. We see it in his departure to a land that he knew not and in his faith as a pilgrim living among the thousands of Canaanites—his faith that said, "This is my land." We see it in his faith in waiting twenty-five years for a son in his old age, against all hope. Abraham even believed God for the raising up of Isaac from the dead on Mount Moriah when he was told to sacrifice him. He was strong in faith, giving glory to God, because he accounted Him who had promised able to perform.

The reason for the weakness of your Christian life is that you try to work it out partly, only allowing God to help you. And that cannot be. You must become utterly helpless, al-

lowing God to work, and God will work gloriously. This is
what we need if we are to truly be workers for God. I could
trace through Scripture and show how Moses, when he led
Israel out of Egypt; how Joshua, when he brought them into
the land of Canaan; how all God's servants in the Old Testament counted upon the omnipotence of God to do the impossible. And this same God lives and is ours today. Yet some
of us still want God to give us a little help while we do our
best, instead of understanding that God wants us to say, "I
can do nothing, God must and will do all." Have you said,
"In worship, in work, in sanctification, in obedience to God,
I can do nothing of myself; my place is to worship the omnipotent God and to believe that He will work in me every
moment"? Oh, may God teach us this! Oh, that God would
by His grace show you what He is like, so worthy of your
trust—an omnipotent God, willing, with His whole omnipotence, to place himself at the disposal of every believer. Shall
we not believe the lesson of the Lord Jesus and say, "Amen;
the things which are impossible with men are possible with
God"?

Apply this lesson to what we have said in previous chapters. We said that the Church must be a Church so set apart
to the Holy Spirit that it has power to set apart men to the
Holy Spirit. And every worker is to be a worker set apart to
the Holy Spirit. That was clearly established from God's Word.
Ah! but has your heart really been expecting that God will
make this true? Do you believe it possible that the everlasting God can say by the Holy Spirit that all the workers in
your church are set apart to the Holy Spirit and they live
day by day like men and women set apart, not for this or
that mission work, but set apart to the Holy Spirit? Can we
expect in the Church of Christ that this life will be a reality?
"The things which are impossible with men are possible with
God." If we fall upon our faces before God and say, "It is
impossible with men, but with God it is possible," God will
honor our faith.

Remember what we said about Peter—his self-confidence, self-power, self-will, and how he came to deny his

Lord. You may have felt: Ah! there is the self-life, there is the flesh-life that rules in me! And now, have you believed that there is deliverance from that? Have you believed that the Almighty God is able to so reveal Christ in your heart, to so call on the Holy Spirit to rule in you, that the self-life shall not have power or dominion over you? Have you coupled the two together and with tears of repentance and deep humiliation and feebleness cried out, "O God, it is impossible for me; man cannot do it, but, glory to Your name, it is possible with God"? Have you claimed deliverance? Come and do it now. Afresh put yourselves in absolute surrender into the hands of a God of infinite love; and as infinite as His love is so is His power to do it.

We also spoke of absolute surrender and felt: This is the great lack in the Church of Christ, this is why the Holy Spirit cannot fill us, and this is why we cannot live as people entirely set apart to the Holy Spirit. Is it any wonder that the flesh and the self-life cannot be conquered? We have never understood what it is to be absolutely surrendered to God like Jesus was. I know many earnest and honest believers who say, "Amen. I accept the message of absolute surrender to God; and yet I tremble and wonder, Will that ever be mine? Can I count upon God to make me one of whom it shall be said in heaven and on earth and in hell, he lives in absolute surrender to God?" Brother, sister, the things which are impossible with men are possible with God. Believe that when He takes charge of you in Christ, it is possible for God to make you a man of absolute surrender. And God is able to maintain that. He can enable you to rise from your bed every morning with the blessed thought directly or indirectly: I am in God's charge; my God is working out my life for me.

Some of you are weary of thinking about sanctification. You pray, you long and cry for it, and yet it appears so far off! The holiness and humility of Jesus—you are so conscious of how distant it is. Beloved friends, the one doctrine of sanctification that is scriptural and real and effectual is: The things which are impossible with men are possible with God. God can sanctify men, and by His almighty and sanctifying power God can keep them. Oh, that you might come a step nearer to your God right now! Oh, that the light of God might shine and you might know your God better before this chapter is finished!

I could go on to what we said about the life of Christ in us—living like Christ, taking Christ as our Savior from sin and as our life and strength. It is God in heaven who can reveal that in you. What does that prayer of the Apostle Paul say: "That he would grant you, according to the riches of his glory"—it must be something very wonderful if it is according to the riches of His glory—"to be strengthened with might by his Spirit in the inner man"? Do you not see that it is an omnipotent God working by His omnipotence in the heart of His believing children, so that Christ can become an indwelling Savior? You may have tried to grasp it, to seize it, to believe it, but it would not come. It was because you had not been brought to believe, "The things which are impossible with men are possible with God."

And I trust that the work spoken about love may have brought you to see: "I must have an inflowing of love in quite a new way; my heart must be filled with life from above, from the fountain of everlasting love, if it is going to overflow all the day; then it will be just as natural for me to love others as it is natural for the lamb to be gentle and the wolf to be cruel." This is the heart condition where the more a man hates and speaks evil of me, the more unlikable and unlovable a man is, I shall love him all the more; the condition where the more obstacles and hatred and ingratitude, the more the power of love triumphs in me. This condition can never be mine until I am brought to say, "It is impossible with men." But if I have been led to say, "This message has spoken to me about a love utterly beyond my power; it is absolutely impossible," then we can come to God and say, "It is possible with God."

Why is it that I speak so specifically regarding your spiritual life? For this one reason: A man or a woman who is to work with power for others must know the power of God in his or her own soul. Let every believer's heart cry out with the earnest prayer: "Lord, may Your Spirit rest upon me and never depart from me. Prove Your mighty power in my soul day by day, in such a way that all men will see that God is almighty to save and to keep."

We desire that our lives might count for God. Dear friends, labor with a joyous face, with a heart full of hope and buoyant expectation. Are you crying to God for a great revival? I can say that that is the unceasing prayer of my heart. Oh, if God would only revive His believing people! When I think of all the unconverted formalists of the Church, or of the infidels and skeptics, or of all the wretched and perishing around me; my heart prays, "My God, revive Your Church and people." I say again, I beseech you by the mercies of God, do pray for God's people. However feeble some believers may be, never mind. If they are children of God they are your brethren. Pray for them, help them out of darkness and out of prison. Pray for God's Church and believe that God is going to give the blessing. Is it for nothing that there is within your heart such yearnings after holiness and consecration? It is a forerunner of God's power. God works *to will* and then He works *to do*. The yearning in your heart, the delight to listen to God's message, the longing for God's blessing, are a witness and a proof that God has worked *to will*. On this basis let us believe that the omnipotent God will work *to do* in us more than we can ask. "Unto him," Paul said, "who is able to do exceeding abundantly above all that we ask or think . . . unto him be glory." Let our hearts say that. Glory to God, the Omnipotent One, who can do above what we dare to ask or think!

Come then with new consecration, with new hope, with new courage, with new joy. Let your heart say: God is with me, Almighty God. I have met with Him and waited for Him. And let it be as it was in Israel: "It shall be said in that day, Lo, this is our God; we have waited for him, and he will save us; this is the Lord, we have waited for him; we will be glad and rejoice in his salvation."

"The things which are impossible with men are possible with God." Surrounding you is a world of sin and sorrow, and the devil is there. Remember, Christ is on the throne, Christ is stronger, Christ has conquered, and Christ will conquer. Go to your work more humble, and empty, and broken, and helpless, and impotent than ever before. Let us praise God that He can work that in every one of us. But wait on Him. My text casts us down: "The things which are *impossible with men*"; but it ultimately lifts us up high—"are *possible with God*." Link yourself to God. Adore and trust God as the Omnipotent One, not only for your own life, but for all the souls that are entrusted to you. Never pray without adoring His omnipotence, and say: "*Mighty God, I claim Your almightiness.*" And the answer to the prayer will come; like Abraham, you will become strong in faith, giving glory to God, because you account Him who hath promised able to perform.

# 11

## *O Wretched Man That I Am!*

*"O wretched man that I am! who shall deliver me from the body of this death? I thank God through Jesus Christ our Lord"* (Rom. 7:24, 25).

Perhaps you realize the wonderful place that this text has in the Epistle to the Romans. It stands here at the end of the seventh chapter as the gateway into the eighth. In the first sixteen verses of the eighth chapter the name of the Holy Spirit is found sixteen times; you have there the description and promise of the life that a child of God can live in the power of the Holy Spirit. This begins in the second verse: "The law of the Spirit of life in Christ Jesus hath made me free from the law of sin and death"; from there Paul goes on to speak of the great privileges of the believer who is led by the Spirit of God. The gateway into all this is in the twenty-fourth verse of the seventh chapter: "O wretched man that I am!" There you have the words of a man who has come to the end of himself. In the previous verses he has described how he had struggled and wrestled in his own power to obey the holy law of God, and had failed. But in answer to his own question he now finds the true answer and cries out: "I thank God through Jesus Christ our Lord." From there he goes on to describe the deliverance that he has found.

From these words I want to describe the path by which a

man can be led out of the spirit of bondage into the spirit of liberty. You know how distinctly it is said: "Ye have not received the spirit of bondage again to fear." We are continually warned that the great danger of the Christian life is to go again into bondage. I want to describe the path by which a man can get out of bondage into the glorious liberty of the children of God. And I want to describe the man himself.

First, these words are the language of a *regenerate* man; second, of an *impotent* man; third, of a *wretched* man, and fourth, of a man *on the border of complete liberty.*

In the first place, then, we have here *the words of a regenerate man.* This is clearly in evidence from the fourteenth verse on to the twenty-third. "It is no more I that do it, but sin that dwelleth in me." That is the language of a regenerate man, a man who knows that his heart and nature have been renewed and that sin is now a power in him that is not himself. "I delight in the law of the Lord after the inward man." That again is the language of a regenerate man. He dares to say when he does evil: "It is no more I that do it, but sin that dwelleth in me." It is of great importance to understand this.

In the first two great sections of the epistle, Paul deals with justification and sanctification. In dealing with justification, he lays the foundation of the doctrine in the teaching about sin, not in the singular, "sin," but in the plural, "sins"— the actual transgressions. In the second part of the fifth chapter he begins to deal with sin, not as actual transgression, but as a power. Just imagine what a loss it would have been if we did not have this second half of the seventh chapter of the Epistle to the Romans if Paul had omitted in his teaching this vital question of the sin in the life of the believer. We would have missed the question we all want answered! What is the answer? The regenerate man is one in whom the will has been renewed and who can say: "I delight in the law of God after the inward man."

Second, *the regenerate man is also an impotent man.* Here

is the great mistake made by many believers. They think that a renewed will is enough, but that is not the case. This regenerate man tells us: I *will* to do what is good, but the power *to perform* I find not. How often people say, You have a new will, and if you determine to obey you can perform what you will. But this man was as determined as any man can be and yet made the confession: "To will is present with me; but how to perform that which is good, I find not."

But, you ask, "Why does God make a regenerate man utter such a confession, with a right will, with a heart that longs to do good, and longs to do its very utmost to love God?" Look at it. Why has God given us our will? Did the angels who fell have the strength to stand in their own will? No. The will of the creature is nothing but an empty vessel in which the power of God is to be made manifest. The creature is meant to find in God all that it is to be. You have it in the second chapter of the Epistle to the Philippians, and you have it here also, that God's work is to work in us both to *will* and to *do* of His good pleasure. Here is a man who appears to say: "God has not worked to *do* in me." But we are taught that God works both to will and to do. How is the apparent contradiction to be reconciled?

You will find that in this passage (7:6–25) the name of the Holy Spirit does not occur. The man is wrestling and struggling to fulfill God's law. In contrast, the law is mentioned nearly twenty times in this section. It describes a believer doing his very best to obey the law of God with his regenerate will. Not only this; but you will find the little words I, me, my occur more than forty times. It is the regenerate "I" in its impotence seeking to obey the law without being filled with the Spirit. This experience is common to nearly every believer. After conversion a man begins to do his best and fails; but if we are brought into the full light we need fail no longer. Nor need we fail at all if we have received the Spirit in His fullness at conversion.

God allows failure so that the regenerate man understands his own utter impotence. It is in the course of this struggle that there comes to us this sense of our utter sinfulness. It is God's way of dealing with us. He allows a man to strive to fulfill the law so that, as he strives and wrestles, he may be brought to this: I am a regenerate child of God, but I am utterly helpless to obey His law. Notice the strong words used all through the chapter to describe this condition: "I am carnal, sold under sin"; "I see another law in my members bringing me into captivity"; and last of all, "O wretched man that I am! who shall deliver me from the body of this death?" The believer who bows here in deep contrition is utterly unable to obey the law of God.

Third, *not only is the man who makes this confession a regenerate and an impotent man, but he is also a wretched man.* He is utterly unhappy and miserable. What is it that makes him so utterly miserable? It is because the life that God has given him loves God so deeply. He is deeply wretched because he feels he is not obeying his God. He says with brokenness of heart: "It is not I that do it, but I am under the awful power of sin which is holding me down. It is I, and yet not I: alas! alas! it is myself; so closely am I bound up with it, and so closely is it intertwined with my very being." Blessed be God when a man learns to say, "O wretched man that I am!" from the depth of his heart. He is on the way to the eighth chapter of Romans.

Many make this confession a pillow for sin. If Paul had to confess his weakness and helplessness in this way, who am I that I should expect to do better? So the call to holiness is quietly set aside. Oh, that each of us had learned to say these words in the very spirit in which they are written here! When we hear sin spoken of as the abominable thing that God hates, do we take it lightly? Would that all Christians who go on sinning and sinning would take this verse to heart. Whenever you utter an unkind word say, "O wretched man that I am!" And every time you lose your temper, kneel down and understand that God never meant you to remain in this condition. Oh, that we would take this word into our daily life and say it every time we defend our own honor, every time we say unkind words, and every time we sin against the Lord God. May we be reminded of the Lord Jesus Christ in His humility, in His obedience, and in His self-sacrifice. Would to God you could forget everything else and cry out, "O wretched man that I am! who shall deliver me from the body of this death?" When a man is brought to this confession, deliverance is at hand.

Remember, it was not only the sense of being impotent and taken captive that made Paul wretched, but above all it was the sense of sinning against his God. The law was doing its work, making sin *exceedingly sinful* in his sight. The thought of continually grieving God became utterly unbearable and brought forth the piercing cry, "O wretched man!" As long as we talk and reason about our impotence and our failure and only try to discover the meaning of Romans 7, it will be of little benefit. But when *every sin* gives new intensity to the sense of wretchedness, when we feel our whole condition as one of not only helplessness but actually exceeding sinfulness, then we shall be pressed not only to ask, Who shall deliver us? but to cry, I thank God through Jesus Christ my Lord.

Fourth, *when a man arrives at this point he is on the very brink of deliverance.* The man has tried to obey the beautiful law of God. He has loved it, he has wept over his sin, he has tried to conquer. He has tried to overcome fault after fault, but every time he has ended in failure. What did Paul mean by "the body of this death"? Did he mean my body when I die? No. In the eighth chapter you have the answer: "If ye through the Spirit do mortify the deeds of the body, ye shall live." That is the body of death from which he is seeking deliverance. And now he is on the brink of deliverance! In the twenty-third verse of the seventh chapter we have the words: "I see another law in my members, warring against the law of my mind, and bringing me into *captivity* to the law of sin which is in my members." It is *a captive* that cries: "O wretched man that I am! who shall deliver me from the body of this death?" He is a man who feels himself bound. But look to the contrast in the second verse of the eighth chapter: "The law of the Spirit of life in Christ Jesus hath *made me free* from the law of sin and death." That is the deliverance through Jesus Christ our Lord; the *liberty* which the Spirit brings to the captive. Can you keep captive a man made free by the "law of the Spirit of life in Christ Jesus"?

But you say, Didn't the regenerate man have the Spirit of Jesus when he spoke in the sixth chapter?

Yes, *but he did not know what the Holy Spirit could do for him.* God does not work by His Spirit as He works by a blind force in nature. He leads His people on as reasonable, intelligent beings. Therefore, when He desires to give us the Holy Spirit whom He has promised, He first brings us to the end of self, to the conviction that though we have been striving to obey the law, we have failed. When we have come to that end, then He shows us that in the Holy Spirit we have the power of obedience, the power of victory, and the power of real holiness.

God works *to will* and He is ready to work *to do,* but, alas! many Christians misunderstand this. They think that because they have the will it is enough and they are able to do it. This is not so. The new will is a permanent gift, an attribute of the new nature. The power to do is not a permanent gift, but must be each moment received from the Holy Spirit. It is the man who is conscious *of his own impotence as a believer* who will learn that by the Holy Spirit *he can live a holy life.* This man is on the brink of that great deliverance; the way has been prepared for the glorious eighth chapter.

I come to you with the solemn thought: Where are you living? Are you saying, "O wretched man that I am! who shall deliver me?" with an occasional experience of the power of the Holy Spirit? Or is it, "I thank God through Jesus Christ"! "the law of the Spirit hath set me free from the law of sin and death"?

What the Holy Spirit does is to give the victory. "If ye through the Spirit do mortify the deeds of the flesh, ye shall live." It is the Holy Spirit who does this—the third Person of the Godhead. He it is who, when the heart is opened wide to receive Him, comes in and reigns there and puts to death the deeds of the body, day by day, hour by hour, and moment by moment.

I want to bring this to a point. Remember, dear friends, that if these thoughts are to do any good, they must bring us to decision and action. There are recorded in Scripture two very different types of believers. The Bible speaks in Romans, Corinthians, and Galatians about those who yield to the flesh; that is the life of tens of thousands of believers. All their lack of joy in the Holy Spirit and lack of the liberty He gives is owing to the flesh. The Spirit is within them, but the flesh rules the life. To be led by the Spirit of God is what they need. I ask you: Have you ever realized what it means that the everlasting God has given His dear Son Christ Jesus to watch over you every day, and that what you have to do is to trust? And that the work of the Holy Spirit is to enable you every moment to remember Jesus and to trust Him? The Spirit has come to keep the link with Him unbroken every moment. Praise God for the Holy Spirit! We are so accustomed to thinking that the Holy Spirit is a luxury, something for special times or for special ministers and men. But the Holy Spirit is necessary for every believer, every moment of the day. Praise God you have Him and that He gives you the full experience of the deliverance in Christ as He makes you free from the power of sin.

Do you long to have the power and the liberty of the Holy Spirit? Bow before God in one final cry of despair: "O God, must I go on sinning this way forever? Who shall deliver me, O wretched man that I am! from the body of this death?" Are you ready to sink before God, in that cry, and seek the power of Jesus to dwell and work in you? Are you ready to say, "I thank God through Jesus Christ"?

What good does it do to attend church or seminars, to study our Bibles and pray, unless our lives are filled with the Holy Spirit? That is what God wants, and nothing else will enable you to live a life of power and peace. You know that when a parent asks his child a question, an answer is expected. Alas! how many believers are content with the ques-

tion put here: "O wretched man that I am! who shall deliver
me from the body of this death?" but never give the answer.
Instead of answering they are silent. Instead of saying, "I
thank God through Jesus Christ our Lord," they are forever
repeating the question without the answer. If you want the
path to the full deliverance of Christ, to the liberty of the
Spirit, to the glorious liberty of the children of God, take it
through the seventh chapter of Romans; and then say, "I
thank God through Jesus Christ our Lord." Do not be content
to remain ever groaning, but say, "I, a wretched man, thank
God, through Jesus Christ. Even though I do not see it all, I
am going to praise God." There is deliverance; there is the
liberty of the Holy Spirit. The kingdom of God *is* "joy in the
Holy Ghost."

# 12

## *Having Begun in the Spirit*

*"This only would I learn of you, Received ye the Spirit by the works of the law, or by the hearing of faith? Are ye so foolish? having begun in the Spirit, are ye now made perfect by the flesh?"* (Gal. 3:2, 3).

When we speak of the quickening or the deepening or the strengthening of the spiritual life, we are thinking of it in relationship to that which is feeble and wrong and sinful. It is a great thing to take our place before God with the honest confession: "O God, our spiritual life is not what it should be!" May God work that in every heart.

As we look at the Church we see so many indications of feebleness, of failure, of sin, and of shortcoming, that we are compelled to ask, How can this be? Is there any necessity for the Church of Christ to be living in such a low condition? Or is it actually possible that God's people should always be living in the joy and strength of their God? Every believing heart must answer, It *is* possible.

Then comes the great question, Why is it, how is it to be accounted for, that God's Church as a whole is so weak and the great majority of believers are not living up to their privileges? There must be a reason for it. Has God not given Christ His Almighty Son to be the keeper of every believer, to make Christ an ever-present reality, and to impart and communicate to us all that we have in Christ? God has given His Son and His Spirit. Why is it that believers do not live up to their privileges?

We find in more than one of the epistles a very solemn answer to that question. There are epistles, such as First Thessalonians, where Paul writes to the believers in effect: I want you to grow, to abound, to increase more and more. They were young, and although there were things lacking in their faith, their condition was satisfactory and gave him great joy. He writes time after time: I pray that you may abound more and more; I write to you to increase more and more. But there are other epistles where he takes a very different tone, especially the epistles to the Corinthians and the Galatians. He tells them in many different ways that the reason they were not living as believers are meant to live is that many of them were under the power of the flesh. My text is one example. He reminds them that by the preaching of faith they had received the Holy Spirit. He had preached Christ to them; they had received Christ and had received the Holy Spirit in power. But what happened? Having begun in the Spirit, they tried to perfect the work that the Spirit had begun by their own fleshly effort. We find the same teaching in the epistles to the Corinthians.

This same solemn discovery is made in the Church of Christ today. God has called the Church of Christ to live in the power of the Holy Spirit, yet the Church is living for the most part in the power of human flesh, of will and energy and effort apart from the Spirit of God. I know this is the case with most believers. If God would use me to give you just one message, it would be this: If the Church will return to acknowledge that the Holy Spirit is her strength and her help, if the Church will return to surrender everything and wait upon God to be filled with the Spirit, her days of beauty and gladness will return and we shall see the glory of God revealed among us. This is my message to every individual believer: Nothing will help you unless you understand that you must live every day under the power of the Holy Spirit. God wants you to be a living vessel in whom the power of the Spirit is to be manifested every hour and every moment of your life, and God will enable you to be that.

Now let us turn our attention to what this word to the Galatians teaches us—some very simple thoughts. It shows us that *the beginning of the Christian life is receiving the Holy Spirit.* It shows us *the great danger of forgetting that we are to live by the Spirit,* and not after the flesh. It shows us what *the fruits and the proofs are of our seeking perfection in the flesh.* And then it suggests to us *the way of deliverance from this condition.*

First of all, Paul says, *"Having begun in the Spirit."* Remember, the Apostle not only preached justification by faith, but he preached something more. He preached—the epistle is full of it—that justified men can only live by the Holy Spirit and that God gives to every justified man the Holy Spirit to seal him. The Apostle says to them more than once: How did you receive the Holy Spirit? Was it by the preaching of the law or by the preaching of faith? He could point back to that time when there had been a mighty revival under his teaching. The power of God had been manifested and the Galatians were compelled to confess: Yes, we received the Holy Spirit—accepting Christ by faith, by faith we received the Holy Spirit.

Unfortunately, it is to be feared that many believers today hardly understand that when they believed, they received the Holy Spirit. Many believers can say: I received pardon and I received peace. But if you were to ask them, Have you received the Holy Spirit? they would hesitate; and some, if they were to say yes, would say it with hesitation. They would also tell you that since that time they have had little understanding of what it is to walk in the power of the Holy Spirit. Let us begin here and take hold of this great truth: The beginning of the true Christian life is to receive the Holy Spirit. This is the work of every Christian minister as it was the work of Paul—to remind his people: Believers, you received the Holy Spirit and you must live according to His guidance and in His power.

If the Galatians who received the Holy Spirit in power were tempted to go astray by that terrible danger of perfecting in the flesh what had been begun in the Spirit, how much more dangerous is it for believers today who barely understand that they have received the Holy Spirit, or who, if they know it as a matter of belief, seldom think of it and seldom praise God for it!

If we are sincerely asking what should be done to have Christ's Church restored, we should begin by accepting the truth that the Holy Spirit must receive a far more honored position among us. In every believer there must be a deep, abiding conviction: What I received from God was not only pardon in heaven, but the Holy Spirit within my heart, to live there and to be my strength.

Second, having begun in the Spirit, *we must see the great danger of forgetting that we are to live by the Spirit.* You are all familiar with railroad switches. A train may be running in a certain direction, but the switches at some place may not be properly opened or closed, and unobservingly the train is switched off to the right or to the left. If that takes place, the train speeds along in the wrong direction and may endanger the lives of all the people on board, whether they realize it or not.

Similarly, God gives the Holy Spirit with the intention that the believer's life would always be lived in the power of the Spirit. A man cannot live a godly life for one hour unless he is empowered by the Holy Spirit. He may live a respectable, consistent life, an irreproachable life, a life of virtue and diligent service. But to live a life acceptable to God, in the enjoyment of God's salvation and God's love, to live and walk in the power of the new life, he cannot unless he is guided by the Holy Spirit every day and every hour.

But now listen to the danger. The Galatians received the Holy Spirit, but what was begun by the Spirit they tried to perfect in the flesh. How? They fell back again under Judaizing teachers who told them they must be circumcised. They began to seek their religion in external observance.

And so Paul uses the expression *"they sought to glory in their flesh"* concerning those teachers who wanted the Galatians circumcised. You sometimes hear the expression *religious flesh*. What is meant by that? It is simply a phrase that expresses the thought: Human nature and human will and human effort can be very active in religion, even after being converted and receiving the Holy Spirit. I may begin in my own strength to try to serve God. I may be very diligent and doing a great deal, and yet all the time doing the work by human strength rather than by God's Spirit. What a solemn thought, that man can, without noticing it, be switched from the line of the Holy Spirit onto the line of the flesh; that he can be working hard and making great sacrifices, and yet it is all in the power of the human will! Ah, the great question for us to ask God in self-examination is that we may be shown whether our life is lived more in the power of the flesh than in the power of the Holy Spirit. A man may be a preacher, he may work energetically in his ministry, others may speak highly of him and of his great sacrifices, and yet you can feel there is something lacking. You feel that he is not a spiritual man; there is little spirituality about his life. How many believers there are about whom no one would ever think of saying, What a spiritual man he is! Ah! this is the weakness of the Church of Christ. It is all in that one word—*flesh*.

Now, the flesh may manifest itself in many ways. It may be manifested in fleshly wisdom. My mind may be very active about spiritual things, I may preach or write or think or meditate or delight in being occupied with things in the Bible and in God's kingdom, and yet the power of the Holy Spirit may be markedly absent. I fear that if you were to evaluate the preaching throughout the Church of Christ and ask, Why is there so little converting power in the preaching of the Word? Why is there so much effort and often so little results for eternity? Why is it that the Word has so little power to build up believers in holiness and in consecration?—the answer will come: It is the absence of the power of the Holy Spirit. Why is this? There can be no other reason but that the flesh and human energy have taken the place of the Holy

Spirit. That was true of the Galatians and the Corinthians. You remember that Paul said to them: I cannot speak to you as to spiritual men; you should be spiritual men, but you are carnal. And you know how often in the course of his Epistles he had to reprove and condemn them for strife and for divisions.

A third thought: *What are the proofs or indications that a church like the Galatians or an individual believer is serving God in the power of the flesh—is perfecting in the flesh what was begun in the Spirit?* The answer is simple. Religious self-effort always ends in sinful flesh. What indicated the condition of the Galatians? They were striving to be justified by the works of the law. And yet they were quarrelling and in danger of devouring one another. Count up the expressions that the Apostle uses to indicate their lack of love and you will find more than twelve—envy, jealousy, bitterness, strife, etc. Read in the fourth and fifth chapters what he says about that. You see how they tried to serve God in their own strength and utterly failed. All this religious effort resulted in failure; the power of sin and the sinful flesh got the better of them, and their whole condition was one of the saddest that could be imagined.

This comes to us with unspeakable solemnity. There is a complaint everywhere in the Christian Church of the lack of a high standard of integrity and godliness, even among professing believers. I remember a sermon which I heard preached by Dr. Dykes on business morality, and he spoke of what was to be found in London. And oh, if the business morality is found to be lacking, what would we discover if we were to go into the homes of Christians! If we think of the life to which God has called His children and promised to enable them to live by the Holy Spirit; if we think of how much, nevertheless, there is of unlovingness and temper and sharpness and bitterness; and if we think of the prevalence of strife among the members of churches, of the envy and jealousy and sensitiveness and pride, then we are compelled to ask, Where are the marks of the presence of the Spirit of the Lamb of God? Sadly lacking, I am afraid!

Many people speak of these fleshly traits as though they were the norm and cannot be helped. Others speak of them as sins, yet have given up the hope of conquering them. Many speak of these things in the Church and do not see the least prospect of ever having them changed. There is no prospect until there comes a radical change, until the Church of God begins to see that every sin in the believer comes from the flesh, even from the fleshly life involved in striving in self-effort to serve God. Until we learn to make confession, until we admit that we must somehow see God's Spirit restored in power in His Church, we must fail. Where did the Church begin in Pentecost? There they began in the Spirit. But, alas, how the Church of the next century veered off into the flesh! They thought to perfect the Church in the flesh.

We should not think that because the blessed Reformation restored the great doctrine of justification by faith, the power of the Holy Spirit was then fully restored. If we believe that God is going to have mercy on His Church in these last days, it will be because the doctrine and the truth about the Holy Spirit will not only be studied, but sought after with a whole heart; and not only because that truth will be sought after, but because ministers and congregations will be found bowing before God in deep abasement with one cry: We have grieved God's Spirit; we have tried to be Christian churches with as little as possible of God's Spirit; we have not sought to be churches filled with the Holy Spirit. Have we faced the awful indictment that the Church of Christ is so powerless because of its refusal to obey its God? That is an awful indictment! The Church redeemed by the blood of Christ, the Church baptized by the Holy Spirit refusing to obey God! And yet it is so.

And why is it so? I know your answer. You say: We are so weak and helpless, we try to obey, we vow to obey, but somehow we fail. Ah yes; *you fail because you do not accept the strength of God.* God alone can work out His will in you. You cannot work out God's will, but His Holy Spirit can. Until the Church, until believers, grasp this and cease trying by human effort to do God's will, waiting upon the Holy Spirit to come with all His omnipotent and enabling power, the Church will never be what God wants her to be and what He is willing to make of her.

I come now to my last thought, the question, *What is the way to restoration?* Beloved friends, the answer is simple. If the train has been mistakenly switched off, there is nothing to do but to come back to the point at which it was misdirected. The Galatians had no other way in returning but to come back to where they had gone wrong, to abandon all religious effort in their own strength and from seeking anything by their own work, and to surrender themselves humbly to the Holy Spirit. There is no other way for us as individuals. Is there within your heart this consciousness: Alas! my life is so lacking in the power of the Holy Spirit? I come to you with God's message: You cannot conceptualize what your life would be in the power of the Holy Spirit. It is too high, too blessed and too wonderful. Nevertheless, just as truly as the everlasting Son of God came to this world and accomplished His wonderful works, just as truly as on Calvary He died and accomplished your redemption by His precious blood, so, just as truly, can the Holy Spirit come into your heart with His divine power to sanctify and enable you to do God's blessed will, filling your heart with joy and strength. But, alas! we have forgotten, we have grieved, we have dishonored the Holy Spirit and He has not been able to do His work. But I bring you the message: The Father in heaven loves to fill His children with His Holy Spirit. God longs to give each of you the power of the Holy Spirit for your daily life. The command comes to us both individually and corporately. God wants us as His children to arise and place our sins before Him, calling upon Him for mercy. Oh, are you so foolish? Having begun in the Spirit, are you perfecting in the flesh that which was begun in the Spirit? Let us bow in shame and confess before God how our fleshly religion, our self-effort and self-confidence, have been the cause of every failure.

I have often been asked by new believers: "Why is it that I so often fail? I did solemnly vow with my whole heart and desire to serve God; why have I failed?" To such I always give the same answer: that they are trying to do in their own strength what Christ alone can do in them. And when I am asked: "I am sure I knew Christ alone could do it. I was not trusting in myself, so how could I fail?" my answer always is that they were trusting in themselves or they could not have failed. If they had trusted Christ, He could not fail. Oh, this perfecting in the flesh what was begun in the Spirit runs far deeper through us than we know. Let us ask God to reveal to us that it is only when we are brought to utter shame and emptiness that we are prepared to receive the blessing that comes from on high.

And so I come with these two questions. Are you living under the power of the Holy Spirit? Are you living as an anointed, Spirit-filled man in your ministry and your life before God? Remember our place is one of solemn responsibility. We are to demonstrate to others what God will do for us, not in our words and teaching, but in our life. God help us to do it! I ask it of every believer: Are you living a life under the power of the Holy Spirit day by day, or are you attempting to live without that? Remember you cannot. Are you consecrated, surrendered to the Spirit to work in you and to live in you? Oh, come and confess every failure of temper, every failure of tongue however small, every failure resulting from the absence of the Holy Spirit and the presence of the power of self. Are you consecrated, are you surrendered to the Holy Spirit?

If your answer is no, then I come with a second question: Are you willing to be consecrated? Are you willing to surrender yourself to the power of the Holy Spirit?

You know very well, I trust, that the human side of consecration will not help you. I may consecrate myself a hundred times with all the intensity of my being, but that will not help me. What will help me is this—that God accepts and seals the consecration.

Are you willing to surrender yourself to the Holy Spirit?

You can do it now. A great deal may still be dark and dim and beyond what we understand, and you may feel nothing; but come. Go into God's presence and meet God himself. God alone can effect the change. God alone, who gave us the Holy Spirit, can restore the Holy Spirit in power into your life. God alone can "strengthen us with might by his Spirit in the inner man." You who have been praying for God's blessing look to God and say: "O God, if You are not with us, nothing will help us." Unless God meets us, we can attend meetings for a month and only receive a little quickening and awakening. Only God can help us permanently. And God will help us if we cast ourselves in helplessness before Him. Oh, let us do so. Let us ask God, that in His great mercy He would visit our souls. Let us, meeting by meeting, step by step, plead with Him: "Lord, come and visit Your Church and let the power of the Holy Spirit be manifested among us." And let us, with the expectation of that, even now say: "Lord I claim for myself and for my fellow believers the presence and the power of the Holy Spirit." To every waiting heart that will make the sacrifice, surrender everything, and give time to cry and pray to God, the answer will come. The blessing is not far off. Our God delights to help us. He will enable us to perfect, not in the flesh, but in the Spirit, what was begun in the Spirit.

# 13

## *Kept by the Power of God*

*"Blessed be the God and Father of our Lord Jesus Christ, which . . . hath begotten us again unto a lively hope by the resurrection of Jesus Christ from the dead, to an inheritance incorruptible . . . reserved in heaven for you, who are kept by the power of God through faith unto salvation"* (1 Pet. 1:3–5).

Here are two wonderful truths about the power by which a believer is kept unto salvation. One truth is, *kept by the power of God*; the other is, *kept through faith*. We want to look at the two sides—at God's side and His mighty power offered to us to be our keeper every moment of the day; and at the human side, our trust in allowing God to do His keeping work. You are begotten again to an inheritance kept in heaven for you; you are kept here on earth by the power of God. A double keeping exists—in heaven *the inheritance is kept for me*, and on earth, *I am kept for the inheritance*.

Now, concerning the first part of this keeping, there is no question. God keeps the inheritance in heaven very wonderfully and perfectly and most safely. Yet the same God keeps me for the inheritance. That is what I want to understand. You know it is very foolish of a father to establish an inheritance for his children, to keep it for them, if he does not keep them for it. Picture a man spending his whole lifetime mak-

ing every sacrifice to amass money, and as he gets his tens
of thousands you ask him why he sacrifices himself so, and
his answer is: I want to leave my children a large inheritance. I am keeping it for them. If you were then to hear that
the same man takes no trouble to educate his children, that
he allows them to run wild in the streets and to go on in
paths of sin and ignorance and folly, what would you think
of him? You would say: How foolish to keep an inheritance
for his children but not keep or prepare his children for the
inheritance. Yet many believers think God is keeping the
inheritance for them; but they cannot believe God is keeping
them for that inheritance. The same power, the same love,
the same God is doing both works.

I want to speak about this work that God does—keeping
us for the inheritance. I have already said that we have two
very simple truths: the one, the divine side—*we are kept by
the power of God*; the other, the human side—*we are kept
through faith*.

First, look at the divine side—*kept by the power of God*.
Think, first of all, that *this keeping is all-inclusive*. What
is kept? *You* are kept. How much of you? Your whole being.
Does God keep one part of you and not another? No. Some
people think in terms of a vague, general keeping; that God
will keep them in such a way that when they die they will
get to heaven. But they do not apply that word *kept* to everything in their being and nature. And yet that is what God
wants. Here I have a watch. Imagine that I had borrowed it
from a friend who said to me, "When you go to Europe I will
let you take it with you, but keep it safe and bring it back."
Now, suppose I injured the watch: The hands were broken,
the face defaced, and some of the wheels and springs destroyed. If I took it back in that condition, my friend would
say, "Ah, but I gave you that watch on the condition that
you would keep it." "Have I not kept it? There is the watch."
"But I did not want you to keep it in that general way, so
that you should bring back only the shell of a watch and its
remains. I expected you to keep every part of it." Similarly,

God does not want to keep us in this general way, so that at the last, somehow or other, we shall be saved as by fire and barely make it into heaven. Rather, the keeping power and the love of God applies to every particular of our being.

Some people think God will keep them in spiritual things, but not in temporal things. This latter, they say, lies outside of His line. But, when God sends you to work in the world, He does not say, "I must now leave while you go and earn your own livelihood." He knows you are not able to keep yourself. Rather, God says, "My child, there is no work you are to do, no business in which you are engaged, and not a penny which you are to spend, but I, your Father, will be with you in My keeping power." God not only cares for the spiritual, but for the temporal also. The greater part of many people's lives must be spent, sometimes eight or nine or ten hours a day, amid the temptations and distractions of business; but God will care for you there. The keeping of God includes all.

There are other people who think that in a time of trial God keeps them, but in times of prosperity they do not need His keeping; then they forget Him and let Him go. Others think the very opposite. They think that in times of prosperity, when things are smooth and quiet, they are able to cling to God, but when heavy trials come, somehow or other their will rebels and God does not keep them. I bring you the message that in prosperity as in adversity, in the sunshine as in the dark, your God is ready to keep you all the time. Yet, there are others who think that God will keep them from doing some great wickedness, but there are small sins they cannot expect God to keep them from. There is the sin of temper. They cannot expect God to conquer that. When you hear of someone who has gone astray or fallen into drunkenness or murder, you thank God for His keeping power. "I might have done the same as that man," you say, "if God had not kept me." And you believe He kept you from drunkenness and murder. So why do you not believe that God can keep you from outbreaks of temper? You thought that this was less important; you did not remember that the great commandment of the New Testament is: "Love one another as I have loved you." And when your temper and hasty judgment and sharp words came out, you sinned against the highest law—the law of God's love. Yet you say, "God will not, God cannot"—no, you will not say "God cannot"; but you say, "God does not keep me from that." You perhaps say, "He can"; yet deep down you feel there is something in you that keeps you from it, and that God does not take it away.

I want to ask you, Can believers live a holier life than is generally lived? Can believers experience the keeping power of God all the day, to keep them from sin? Can believers be kept in fellowship with God? I bring you a message from the Word of God, *kept by the power of God*. There is no qualifying clause to these words. The meaning is that if you will entrust yourself entirely and absolutely to the omnipotence of God, He will delight to keep you.

Some people do not believe it possible that every word of their mouth should be to the glory of God. But it is what God desires, indeed it is what God expects from them. God is willing to place a guard at the door of their mouth, and if He will do that, can He not keep their tongue and their lips? He can; that is what God is going to do for those who trust Him. God's keeping is all-inclusive, and I want everyone who desires to live a holy life to think about all their weaknesses, all their shortcomings, all their sins, and to say deliberately: "Is there any sin or weakness that my God could not keep me from?" And the heart will have to answer: "No. God can keep me from each of these."

Secondly, if you want to understand this keeping, remember that it is not only an all-inclusive keeping, but it is an *almighty keeping*. I want that truth burned into my soul. I want to worship God until my whole heart is filled with the thought of His omnipotence. God is almighty, and the Almighty God offers himself to work in my heart, to do the work of keeping me. I want to get linked with Omnipotence, or rather, linked to the Omnipotent One, to the living God, and to have my place in the hollow of His hand. As you read the Psalms, think of the wonderful thoughts in many of David's expressions: for instance, when he speaks about God being *our God, our fortress, our refuge, our strong tower, our strength,* and *our salvation.* David had very wonderful views of how the everlasting God himself is the hiding place of the believing soul, and of how He takes the believer and keeps him in the very hollow of His hand, in the secret of His pavilion, under the shadow of His wings, under His very feathers. And there David lived. Yet, we who are the children of Pentecost, we who have known Christ and His blood and the Holy Spirit sent down from heaven, why is it we know so little of what it is to walk step by step with the Almighty God as our keeper?

Have you ever considered that in every action of grace in your heart, you have the whole omnipotence of God working to bless you? When a man gives me a gift of money, I receive it and go away with it. He has given me something of his; the rest he keeps for himself. But that is not how it is with the power of God. God can part with nothing of His own power; therefore I can experience the power and goodness of God only to the extent that I am in contact and fellowship with Him. When I come into contact and fellowship with Him, I come into contact and fellowship with the whole omnipotence of God and have the omnipotence of God to help me every day. Think of a son who has a very rich father, and as the son is about to open his own business the father says, "You can have as much money as you want for your undertaking." All the father has is at the disposal of his son. That is the way with God, your Almighty God. It is almost beyond our imagination; we feel like such a little worm. His omnipotence needed to keep a little worm! Yes, His omnipotence is needed to keep every little worm that lives in the dust, and also to keep the universe, and therefore His omnipotence is much more needed in keeping your soul and mine from the power of sin.

Oh, if you want to grow in grace, learn to begin here: in all your judgings and meditations and thoughts and deeds and questionings and studies and prayers, learn to be kept by your Almighty God. What is Almighty God not going to do for the child that trusts Him? The Bible says, "Above all that we can ask or think." When you learn to know and trust Him in His power, then you will live as a believer should. How little we have learned to study God, and to understand that a godly life is a life full of God, a life that loves God and waits on Him, and trusts Him and allows Him to bless it! We can do the will of God only by the power of God. God gives us the first experience of His power to prepare us to desire more and to come and claim all that He can do. God help us to trust Him every day.

Another thought. *This keeping is* not only all-inclusive and omnipotent, but also *continuous and unbroken.* People sometimes say, "For a week or a month God has kept me very wonderfully. I have lived in the light of His countenance and cannot tell what joy I have had in fellowship with Him. He has blessed me in my work for others. Lives have been changed and at times I felt as if I were carried heavenwards on eagle wings. But it did not continue. It was too good to last." Some say, "It was necessary that I should fall to keep me humble." Others say, "I know it was my own fault; but somehow you cannot always live up in the heights." O beloved, why is it? Can there be any reason why the keeping of God should not be continuous and unbroken? Just think. All life is in unbroken continuity. If my heart were stopped for half an hour, I would be dead and my life gone. Life is continuous, and the life of God is the life of His Church and His almighty power working in us. God comes to us as the Almighty One, and without any condition He offers to be our keeper. His keeping means that day by day, moment by moment, He is going to keep us.

If I were to ask you: "Do you think God is able to keep you one whole day from actual transgression?" some of you would answer: "I not only know He is able to do it, but I think He has done it. There have been days in which He has kept my heart in His holy presence and kept me from conscious, actual transgression." Now, if He can do that for a minute or an hour or a day, why not for two days? Oh! let us make God's omnipotence as revealed in His Word the measure of our expectations. Has God not said in His Word, "I, the Lord, do keep it, and will water it, every moment"? What can that mean? Does "every moment" mean every moment? Did God promise of that vineyard of red wine that *every moment* He would water it so that the heat of the sun and the scorching wind might never dry it up? Yes. In South Africa when they graft branches together, they sometimes tie a bottle of water above it so that now and then a drop of water will saturate what they have joined together. The moisture is kept there unceasingly until the graft has had time to fully join together and resist the heat of the sun. Will our God, in His tenderhearted love toward us, not keep us every moment when He has promised to do so? Oh! if we could only see that our whole life is to be God's doing: "It is God that worketh in us to will and to do of his good pleasure." When we finally exercise faith to expect this from God, God will do all for us.

The keeping is to be continuous. Every morning God will meet you as you awaken. There is no question about it. If you trust God, He will meet you as you awaken in the morning with His divine sunshine and love. He will give you the consciousness: Today I have God to keep me continuously with His almighty power. And God will meet you the next day and every day; never mind if in the practice of fellowship there comes occasional failure. If you maintain your position and say: "Lord, I am going to expect You to do Your utmost and I am going to trust You day by day to keep me absolutely," your faith will grow stronger and stronger and you will know the keeping power of God in unbrokenness.

Now for the other side—*believing.* "Kept by the power of God *through faith.*" How should we understand this faith?

Let me say, first of all, that this *faith means utter powerlessness and helplessness before God.* At the bottom of all faith there is a feeling of helplessness. If I am in the process of buying a house, I entrust a legal agent with the work of getting the transfer of the property into my name and making all the legal arrangements. I cannot do that work, and in trusting that agent I confess I cannot do it. Similarly, faith always means helplessness. Sometimes it means: I can do it with a great deal of trouble, but another can do it better. But in most cases it is utter helplessness; *another must do it for me.* And that is the secret of the spiritual life. A man must learn to say: I surrender everything; I have tried and desired, thought and prayed, but failure has come. God has blessed and helped me, but still, in the long run, there has been so much of sin and sadness. What a change comes when a man is broken down into utter helplessness and self-despair and says: I can do nothing!

Remember Paul. He was living a blessed life, he had been taken up into the third heaven, and then the thorn in the flesh came, "a messenger of Satan to buffet him." And what happened? Paul could not understand it, so he prayed that the Lord would take it away; but the Lord said, in effect: No; it is possible you might exalt yourself. Therefore I have sent you this trial to keep you weak and humble. Paul then learned a lesson that he never forgot—to rejoice in his infirmities. He said that the weaker he was the better it was for him, for when he was weak he was strong in his Lord Christ.

Do you want to enter what people call "the higher life"? Then go a step lower down. I remember Dr. Boardman telling about visiting a factory to observe a new technological system. To view the operation, his friend wanted to take Dr. Boardman up to the top of the tower to see how the work was done. The doctor came to the tower, entered by the door and began going upstairs; but when he had gone a few steps his friend called out, "That is the wrong way. You must come down this way; that stair is locked up." The gentleman took him down a long stairs and there a lift was ready to take him to the top; he said, "Here is a lesson that going down is often the best way to get up." Ah yes, God will have to bring us down very low; there will have to come upon us a sense of emptiness and despair and nothingness. It is when we sink down in utter helplessness that the everlasting God will reveal himself in His power and that our hearts will learn to trust God alone.

What is it that keeps us from trusting Him perfectly?

Many say, "I believe what you say, but there is one difficulty. If my trust were perfect and always abiding, all would be right, for I know God will honor trust. But how am I to get that trust?" By the death of self. The great hindrance to trust is self-effort. As long as you have your own wisdom and thoughts and strength, you cannot fully trust God. But when God breaks you down, when everything begins to grow dim before your eyes and you see that you understand nothing, then God is coming near. If you will bow down in nothingness and wait upon God, He will become all. *As long as we are something, God cannot be all,* and His omnipotence cannot do its full work. That is the beginning of faith—utter despair of self, a ceasing from man and everything on earth, and finding our hope in God alone.

Next, we must understand that *faith is rest.* In the beginning of the faith-life, faith is struggling; but as long as faith is struggling, faith has not attained its strength. But when faith in its struggling comes to the end of itself and just casts itself upon God and rests on Him, then comes joy and victory.

Perhaps I can clarify this if I tell the story of how the Keswick Convention began. Canon Battersby was an evangelical clergyman of the Church of England for more than twenty years, a man of deep and tender godliness, but he did not have the consciousness of rest and of victory over sin, and often was deeply sad at the thought of stumbling and failure and sin. When he heard about the possibility of victory, he truly desired it but it was as if he could not reach it. On one occasion, he heard a message on rest and faith from the story of the nobleman who came from Capernaum to Cana to ask Christ to heal his child. In the message it was shown that the nobleman believed that Christ could help him in a general way, but he really came to Jesus by way of an experiment. He hoped Christ would help him, but he was not convinced of that help. But what happened? When Christ said to him, "Go thy way, for thy child liveth," that man believed the word that Jesus spoke; he rested in that word. He had no proof that his child was well and had a return walk of seven hours journey to Capernaum. He walked back and on the way met his servant who brought the first news that the child was well. At one o'clock on the afternoon of the previous day, at the very time that Jesus had spoken to him, the fever had left the child. That father rested upon the word of Jesus and His work, and he went down to Capernaum and found his child well; he praised God and became with his whole house a believer and a disciple of Jesus. Oh, friends, that is faith! When God comes to me with the promise of His keeping and I have nothing on earth to trust in, I say to God, "Your word is enough"; "kept by the power of God." That is faith, that is rest.

After Canon Battersby heard that message, he went home and in the darkness of the night found rest. He rested on the word of Jesus. The next morning, in the streets of Oxford, he said to a friend, "I have found it!" Then he went and told others and asked that the Keswick Convention might be started and that those at the Convention along with himself should testify simply to what God had done.

It is a great thing when a man comes to rest on God's almighty power for every moment of his life, in regards to temptations to temper, haste, anger, unlovingness, pride and sin. It is a great thing to enter into a covenant with the omnipotent Jehovah, not on account of anything that any man says or his heart feels, but on the strength of the Word of God: "Kept by the power of God through faith." Oh, let us say to God that we are going to prove Him to the very uttermost. Let us say: "We ask You for nothing more than You can give, but we want nothing less." Let us say: "My God, let my life be a proof of what the omnipotent God can do." Let these be the two dispositions of our souls every day—deep helplessness and simple, childlike rest.

One more thought in regard to faith—*faith implies fellowship with God.* Many people want to take the Word and believe that, but they find they cannot believe it. Ah no! you cannot separate God from His Word. No goodness or power can be received separate from God; and if you want to get into this life of godliness, you *must* take time for fellowship with God.

People sometimes tell me, "My life is so hurried and busy that I have no time for fellowship with God." A dear missionary said to me, "People do not know how we missionaries are tempted. I get up at five o'clock in the morning and there are the nationals waiting for their orders for work. Then I have to go to school and spend hours there; and then there is other work. Sixteen hours rush along and I hardly get time to be alone with God." Ah! there is the problem. I want you to remember two things. I have not told you to trust the omnipotence of God as a thing, and I have not told you to trust the Word of God as a written book, but I have told you to go to the God of omnipotence and the God of the Word. Deal with God as that nobleman dealt with the living Christ. Why was he able to believe the word that Christ spoke to him? Because in the very eyes and tones and voice of Jesus, the Son of God, he saw and heard something which caused him to feel that he could trust Him. And that is what Christ can do for you and me. Do not try to stir and arouse faith from within. How often I have tried to do that and made a fool of myself! You cannot stir up faith from the depths of your heart. Leave your heart and look into the face of Christ and listen to what He tells you about how He will keep you. Look up into the face of your loving Father. Take time every day with Him and begin a new life with the deep emptiness and poverty of a man who has nothing and who waits to receive everything from Him; with the deep restfulness of a man who rests on the living God, the omnipotent Jehovah; and prove Him if He will not open the windows of heaven and pour out a blessing too large to contain it.

I close by asking you if you are willing to fully experience the heavenly keeping for the heavenly inheritance. Robert Murray M'Cheyne said, "O God, make me as holy as a pardoned sinner can be made." And, if you will say that earnestly, from the depths of your heart, come and enter into a covenant with the everlasting and omnipotent Jehovah afresh, and in great helplessness, but in great restfulness, place yourself into His hands. And then as you enter into your covenant, take with you the promise that the everlast-

ing God is going to be your companion, holding your hand
every moment of the day. Our keeper is watching over us
without a moment's interval; our Father is delighting to reveal himself in our souls always. He has the power to let the
sunshine of His love shine on us all the day. Do not be afraid
that because you have a secular job, you cannot have God
with you always. Learn a lesson from the natural sun which
shines upon you all day and you enjoy its light; and wherever
you are, God takes care that it shines upon you. And God
will take care that His own divine light shines upon you and
that you shall abide in that light if you will only trust Him
for it. Let us trust God to do that with a great and entire
trust.

Listen to these last words. Here is the omnipotence of
God, and here is faith reaching out to the measure of that
omnipotence. Shall we not say, "All that that omnipotence
can do, I am going to trust my God for"? Are not the two
sides of this heavenly life wonderful? God's omnipotence covering me, and my will in its littleness resting in that omnipotence and rejoicing in it!

> Moment by moment, I'm kept in His love;
> Moment by moment, I've life from above;
> Looking to Jesus, the glory doth shine;
> Moment by moment, O Lord, I am Thine!

# 14

## *Ye Are the Branches*

In this final chapter my desire is to speak especially to Christian workers. The one thought in my heart is this— that everything depends on our being in a right relationship with Jesus Christ. If I want good apples, I must have a good apple tree; and if I care for the health of the apple tree, the apple tree will give me apples. The same is true with our Christian work. *If our life with Christ is right,* all will come right. There may be the need of instruction and suggestion and help and training in the different areas of the work; all that has its proper value. But in the long run, the greatest essential is to have our full life in Christ; in other words, to have Christ in us working through us. And I pray that God may comfort and encourage every beloved servant of His. I know how much there is that often disturbs us or causes anxious questionings; but the Master has such a blessing for each of us, such perfect peace and rest, and such joy and strength, if we can only enter into and abide in the right attitude toward Him.

I have taken my thoughts from the parable of the Vine and the Branches in John 15:5: *"I am the vine, ye are the branches."* I want to consider especially the words, *"Ye are the branches."*

What a simple thing it is to be a branch of a tree or vine! The branch grows out of the vine or the tree, and there it lives and grows, and, in due time, bears fruit. It has no responsibility except to receive from the root and stem sap and nourishment. Similarly, if by the Holy Spirit we understood our relationship to Jesus Christ, our work would be transformed into the brightest and most heavenly thing upon earth. Instead of always being weary or exhausted, our work would be like a new experience, linking us to Jesus as nothing else can. After all, isn't it true that our work often comes between us and Jesus? What folly! The very work that He has to do in us, and we for Him, we take up in such a way that it separates us from Christ. Many workers in the vineyard have complained that they have too much work and not enough time for close communion with Jesus; that his normal work decreases his inclination for prayer and that his intense involvement with men darkens the spiritual life. Sad thought, that the bearing of fruit should separate the branch from the vine! Surely this is because we have looked upon our work as something other than the branch bearing fruit. May God deliver us from every false thought about the Christian life.

Now, just a few thoughts about this blessed branch-life.

In the first place, it is *a life of absolute dependence*. The branch has nothing; it just depends upon the vine for everything. That word *absolute dependence* is a most solemn and precious word. A great German theologian wrote two large volumes some years ago to show that the whole of Calvin's theology is summed up in that one principle of *absolute dependence upon God;* and he was right. Another great writer has said that *absolute, unalterable dependence upon God alone* is the essence of the religion of angels and should be that of men also. God is everything to the angels and is willing to be everything to the believer. If I can learn every moment of the day to depend upon God, everything will come right. You will receive the higher life if you depend absolutely upon God.

Now, here we find it with the vine and the branches. Every vine you see and every cluster of grapes that comes upon your table, let them remind you that the branch is absolutely dependent on the vine. The vine does the work while the branch enjoys the fruit of it.

What must the vine do? It has to do a great work. It has to send its roots out into the soil and hunt under the ground—the roots often extend far out—for nourishment and to drink in the moisture. Put certain fertilizers in certain directions and the vine sends its roots there; then in its roots or stems it turns the moisture and fertilizer into that special sap which produces the fruit to be borne. The vine does the work and the branch simply has to receive from the vine the sap, which is changed into grapes. I have been told that at Hampton Court there was a vine that sometimes bore a couple of thousand clusters of grapes. People were astonished at its large growth and rich fruitage. Afterward it was discovered that not so very far away runs the River Thames, and the vine had stretched its roots hundreds of yards under the ground until it had come to the riverside. There, in all the rich slime of the riverbed, it had found rich nourishment, obtained moisture, and the roots had drawn the sap all that distance up into the vine, resulting in an abundant and rich harvest. The vine had the work to do and the branches simply had to depend upon the vine and receive what it gave.

Is that not literally true of my Lord Jesus? Should I understand that when I must work, when I have to preach a sermon or teach a Bible class, or go out and visit the poor neglected ones, all the responsibility of the work is on Christ?

That is exactly what Christ desires you to understand. Christ desires that in all your work, the very foundation should be the simple, blessed consciousness: Christ must care for all.

And *how does He fulfill the trust of that dependence?* He does it by sending down the Holy Spirit—not now and then as a special gift, for remember that there is a vital relation between the vine and the branches by which hourly, daily and unceasingly a living connection is maintained. The sap does not flow for a time and then stop and then flow again, but from moment to moment the sap flows from the vine to the branches. And in like manner, my Lord Jesus wants me to take that blessed position as a worker. Morning by morning, day by day, hour by hour, step by step, and in every work I must do, simply to abide before Him in the utter helplessness of one who knows nothing, and is nothing, and can do nothing. Oh, beloved workers, study that word *nothing*. You sometimes sing, "Oh, to be nothing, nothing"; but have you really studied that word, and prayed every day, and worshiped God in the light of it? Do you know the blessedness of that word *nothing*?

If I am something, then God is not everything; but when I become *nothing*, God can become *all* and the everlasting God in Christ can reveal himself fully. That is the higher life. We need to become nothing. Someone has well said that the seraphim and cherubim are flames of fire because they know they are nothing and they allow God to put His fullness and His glory and brightness into them. They are nothing, and God is all in them and around them. Oh, become nothing in deep reality, and, as a worker, study only one thing—to become poorer and lower and more helpless, that Christ may work all in you.

Workers, here is your first lesson: Learn to be nothing, learn to be helpless. The man who has something is not absolutely dependent; but the man who has nothing is absolutely dependent. Absolute dependence upon God is the secret of all power in work. The branch has nothing but what it receives from the vine, and you and I can have nothing except what we receive from Jesus.

The second thought is that the life of the branch is not only a life of entire dependence, but *of deep restfulness*. Oh, that little branch, if it could think and speak—that branch away in Hampton Court vine—if we could ask that little branch, "Come, branch of the vine, tell me, I want to learn from you how I can be a true branch of the living Vine," what would it answer? The little branch would whisper: "Man, I hear that you are wise and I know that you can do many wonderful things. I know you have been given much strength and wisdom, but I have one lesson for you. With all your hurry and effort in Christ's work you never prosper. The first thing you need is to come and rest in your Lord Jesus. That is what I do. Since I grew out of the vine I have spent years and years, and all I have done is simply to rest in the vine. When the time of spring came I had no anxious thought or care. The vine began to pour its sap into me to give to the bud and leaf. When the time of summer came I had no care, and in the great heat I trusted the vine to bring moisture to keep me fresh. In the time of harvest, when the owner came to pluck the grapes, I had no care. If there was anything not good in the grapes, the owner never blamed the branch; the blame was always on the vine. And if you would be a true branch of Christ, the living Vine, just rest on Him. Let Christ bear the responsibility."

You say: Won't that make me slothful? I tell you it will not. No one who learns to rest upon the living Christ can become slothful, for the closer your contact with Christ, the more of the Spirit of His zeal and love will be borne in upon you. But oh, begin to work into the midst of your entire dependence the addition of *deep restfulness*. A man sometimes tries and tries to be dependent upon Christ, but he worries himself about this absolute dependence; he tries and he cannot get it. But let him sink down into entire restfulness every day.

> In Thy strong hand I lay me down,
>   So shall the work be done;
> For who can work so wondrously
>   As the Almighty One?

Worker, take your place every day at the feet of Jesus, in the blessed peace and rest that come from the knowledge—

> I have no care, my cares are His;
> I have no fear, He cares for all my fears.

Come, children of God, and understand that it is the Lord Jesus who wants to work through you. You complain of the lack of fervent love. It will come from Jesus. He will pour the divine love into your heart with which you can love people. That is the meaning of the assurance, "The love of God is shed abroad in our hearts by the Holy Spirit"; and of that other word, "The love of Christ constraineth us." Christ can give you such a fountain of love that you cannot help but love the most wretched, the most ungrateful, or those who have wearied you the most. Rest in Christ who can give wisdom and strength—you do not realize how that restfulness will often prove to be the very best part of your message. You plead and argue with people and give them the idea that you are arguing and striving with them. They only feel as if two men are dealing with each other. But if you will let the deep rest of God come over you, the rest in Christ Jesus, the peace and rest and holiness of heaven, that restfulness will bring a blessing to the heart, even more than the words you speak.

In the third thought, *the branch teaches a lesson of much fruitfulness.* You know that the Lord Jesus repeated the word *fruit* often in that parable. He spoke, first, of *fruit,* then of *more fruit,* and then of *much fruit.* Yes, you are ordained not only to bear fruit, but to bear *much fruit.* "Herein is my Father glorified, *that ye bear much fruit."* In the first place, Christ said, "I am the vine, and my Father is the husbandman." My Father is the Husbandman who has charge of Me and you. He who will watch over the connection between Christ and the branches is God; and it is in the power of God through Christ we are to bear fruit.

O believer, you know the world is perishing for the lack of workers. And it needs not only more workers. The workers are saying, some more earnestly than others: "We need not only more workers, but our workers need to have a new power, a different life; then we shall be able to bring more blessing." Child of God, I appeal to you. Think of the trouble you take, say, in a case of sickness. You have a friend who is apparently in danger of death, and nothing can save that friend except a medicine which is very rare. Think of the trouble you would take to find a source for this medicine to save this dying friend! Yet all around us are millions of people who never go to a church or who may go to church but do not know Christ. And the only salvation is the heavenly grapes, the grapes of Eshcol, the grapes of the heavenly Vine. These are impossible to buy at any price unless believers bear them out of their inner life in fellowship with Christ. Unless the children of God are filled with the sap of the heavenly Vine, unless they are filled with the Holy Spirit and the love of Jesus, they cannot bear much of the real heavenly grape. We all confess there is a great deal of work, a great deal of preaching and teaching and visiting, a great deal of earnest effort of every kind; but there is so little manifestation of the power of God in all of it.

What is the problem? There is a lack in the close connection between the worker and the heavenly Vine. Christ, the heavenly Vine, has blessings that He could pour on tens of thousands who are perishing. Christ, the heavenly Vine, has power to provide the heavenly grapes. But "ye are the branches," and you cannot bear heavenly fruit unless you are in a vital relationship with Jesus Christ.

Do not confuse work and fruit. There may be a good deal of work for Christ that is not the fruit of the heavenly Vine. Do not seek for work only. Oh! study this question of fruit bearing. It means the very life, power, Spirit, and love within the heart of the Son of God—it means the heavenly Vine himself coming into your heart and mine.

You know there are different sorts of grapes. From country to country there are many kinds, each with a different name. And every vine provides exactly that peculiar aroma and juice which gives the grape its particular flavor and taste. Likewise, there is in the heart of Christ Jesus a life, a love, a Spirit, a blessing, and a power for men that is entirely heavenly and divine, and that will come down into our hearts. Stand in close connection with the heavenly Vine and say: "Lord Jesus, nothing less than the sap that flows through yourself, nothing less than the Spirit of Your divine life is what I ask. Lord Jesus, let Your Spirit flow through me in all my work for You." I tell you again that the sap of the heavenly Vine is nothing but the Holy Spirit. The Holy Spirit is the life of the heavenly Vine. What you must receive from Christ is nothing less than a strong inflowing of the Holy

Spirit. You need it desperately, but you need nothing more than that. Remember that. Do not expect Christ to give a bit of strength here and a bit of blessing there. As the vine does its work in giving its own peculiar sap to the branch, so expect Christ to give His own Holy Spirit into your heart and then you will bear much fruit. If you have only begun to bear fruit and are listening to the word of Christ in the parable, "more fruit," "much fruit," remember that in order to bear more fruit you simply need more of Jesus in your life and heart.

We ministers of the gospel, how we are in danger of getting into a condition of *work, work, work*! And we pray about it, but the freshness and buoyancy and joy of the heavenly life are not always present. Let us seek to understand that the life of the branch is a life of much fruit because it is a life rooted in Christ, the living, heavenly Vine.

The fourth thought addresses the truth that *the life of the branch is a life of close communion.* Let us ask again, What does the branch have to do? You know that precious inexhaustible word that Christ used: *abide.* Your life is to be an abiding life. And what is the abiding like? It is to be just like the branch in the vine, abiding every minute of the day. There are the branches, in close communion, in unbroken communion, with the vine, from January to December. And can't I live every day (to me it is almost a terrible thing that we should ask the question) in abiding communion with the heavenly Vine? You say, "But I am so much occupied with other things." You may have ten hours of hard work daily, during which you are occupied with temporal things; God is fully aware of this. But the abiding work is the work of the *heart,* not of a physical location, the work of the heart clinging to and resting in Jesus, a work in which the Holy Spirit links us to Christ Jesus. Believe that deep down in the inner life you can abide in Christ, so that every moment you are free to realize: "Blessed Jesus, I am still in You." If you will learn for a time to put aside other work and to get into this abiding contact with the heavenly Vine, you will find that fruit will come.

What is the application to our life with regard to this abiding communion? What does it mean? It means close fellowship with Christ in private prayer. I am sure there are believers who do long for the higher life, who occasionally receive a great blessing, and have at times found a great inflow of heavenly joy and a great outflow of heavenly gladness; and yet after a time it has passed away. They have not understood that close personal communion with Christ is an absolute necessity for daily life. Take time to be alone with Christ. Nothing in heaven or earth can free you from the necessity for that if you are to be joyous and holy.

Oh! how many believers look upon it as a burden, a duty, and a difficulty to get alone with God! That is the great hindrance to Christian lives everywhere. We need more quiet fellowship with God. I tell you in the name of the heavenly Vine that you cannot be a healthy branch, a branch into which the heavenly sap can flow, unless you take plenty of time for communion with God. If you are not willing to sacrifice time to get alone with Him, to give Him time every day to work in you, to keep up the link of connection between you and himself, He cannot give you that blessing of His unbroken fellowship. Jesus Christ asks you to live in close communion with Him. Let every heart say: "O Christ, it is this I long for, it is this I choose." And He will gladly give it to you.

And then my last thought. *The life of the branch is a life of entire surrender.* This word, *entire surrender,* is a great and solemn work, and I believe we do not understand its meaning. Still the little branch preaches it. "Have you anything to do, little branch, besides bearing grapes?" "No, *nothing.*" "Are you fit for nothing?" Fit for nothing! The Bible says that a piece of vine cannot even be used as a pen; it is fit for nothing but to be burned. "And now, what do you understand, little branch, about your relation to the vine?" "My relation is just this: I am utterly surrendered to the vine, and the vine can give me as much or as little sap as it chooses. Here I am at its disposal, and the vine can do with me what it likes."

Oh, friends, we need this entire surrender to the Lord Jesus Christ. The more I minister, the more I feel that this is one of the most difficult points to make clear and one of the most important and needful points to explain—what this entire surrender is. It is often easy for a person to come and offer himself to God for entire consecration and say, "Lord, it is my desire to give myself entirely to You." That is of great value and often brings very rich blessing. But the one question I should study quietly is: What is *meant* by entire surrender? It means that just as literally as Christ was surrendered entirely to God, you are surrendered entirely to Christ. Is that too strong? Some of you think so. Some think that never can be; that just as entirely and absolutely as Christ yielded His life to do nothing but seek the Father's pleasure and to depend on the Father absolutely and entirely, we are to do nothing but seek the pleasure of Christ. But that is actually true. Christ Jesus came to breathe His own Spirit into us, to make us find our very highest happiness in living entirely for God, just as He did. Oh, beloved, if that is the case, then I should say: Yes, as true as it is of that little branch of the vine, so true, by God's grace, I want it to be of me. I would live day by day that Christ may be able to do with me what He desires.

Ah! here comes the terrible mistake that lies at the bottom of so much of religion. A man thinks: I have my business, my family duties, my responsibilities as a citizen, and all this cannot change. And now alongside all this I am to take in the service of God as something that will keep me from sin. God help me to perform my duties properly! That is not right. When Christ came, He came and bought the sinner with His blood. If there was a slave market here and I were to buy a slave, I could take that slave to my own house and he would live as my personal property and I could give him orders all day long. If he were a faithful slave, he would live as having no will and no interests of his own, his one care being to promote the well-being and honor of his master. In like manner I, who have been bought with the blood of Christ, have been bought to live every day with the one thought: How can I please my Master?

We find the Christian life so difficult because we seek for God's blessing while we live the Christian life according to our own desire. We make our own plans and choose our own work, and then we ask the Lord Jesus to come in and take care that sin shall not conquer us too much and that we shall not go too far wrong; we ask Him to come in and give us so much of His blessing. But our relation to Jesus should be such that we are entirely at His disposal, coming to Him every day humbly and straightforwardly and saying: "Lord, is there anything in me that is not according to Your will, that has not been ordered by You, or that is not entirely surrendered to You?" If we would wait, and wait patiently, I tell you what the result would be. There would spring up a relationship between us and Christ so close and so tender that we would be amazed at how we formerly could have lived with the idea: I am surrendered to Christ. We will realize how distant our fellowship with Him had previously been, and that He can, and does indeed come to take actual possession of us and give unbroken fellowship all the day. The branch calls us to entire surrender.

I am not speaking now about the need to surrender our sins. It may be that you need to do that: perhaps a violent temper, a bad habit, and actual sins that have never been given up into the very bosom of the Lamb of God. I pray you, if you are a branch of the living Vine, do not keep one sin back. I know that many do not think exactly as I do on this question of holiness, but that would be a matter of comparative indifference if I could see that all are honestly longing to be free from every sin. But I am afraid that unconsciously many compromise with the idea: We cannot be without sin, we must sin a little every day; we cannot help it. Oh, that people would actually cry to God: "Lord, keep me from sin!" Yield yourself completely to Jesus and ask Him to do His very utmost in keeping you from sin.

I said I would not speak about sin; but oh! there is so much worldliness in our work, in our Church and our surroundings that we have grown used to it and we think: That is all right; it cannot be changed anyway. We do not come to the Lord Jesus and ask Him about it. Oh! I advise you, *bring everything into relationship with Jesus* and say: "Lord, everything in my life has to be in complete harmony with my position as a branch of Yours, the blessed Vine." Let your surrender to Christ be entire. I do not fully understand that word *surrender*; it receives new meanings now and then; it enlarges immensely from time to time. But I advise you to speak it out: "Absolute surrender to You, O Christ, is what I have chosen." And Christ will show you what is not according to His mind and lead you on to deeper and higher blessedness.

In conclusion, let me gather it all up in one word. Christ Jesus said, "I am the vine, ye are the branches." In other words: "I, the living One who have so completely given myself to you, am the Vine. You cannot trust Me too much. I am the Almighty Worker, full of a divine life and power." Believer, you are the branch of the Lord Jesus Christ. If there is in your heart the consciousness: I am not a strong, healthy, fruit-bearing branch, I am not closely linked with Jesus, I am not living in Him as I should be—then listen to Him saying: "I am the Vine, I will receive you, I will draw you to myself, I will bless you, I will strengthen you, I will fill you with My Spirit. I, the Vine, have taken you to be My branch. I have given myself utterly to you; child, give yourself utterly to Me. I have surrendered myself as God absolutely to you. I became Man and died for you that I might be entirely yours. Come and surrender yourself entirely to be Mine."

What is your answer? Let it be the prayer from the depths of your heart that the living Christ may link you close to himself. Let your prayer be that He, the living Vine, shall link you so close to himself that your heart will sing: He is my Vine, and I am His branch—I want nothing more—now I have the everlasting Vine. Then, when you get alone with Him, worship and adore Him, praise and trust Him, love Him and wait for His love: "You are my Vine, and I am Your branch. It is enough, my soul is satisfied." Glory to His blessed name!